ŚIVASTOTRĀVALĪ OF UTPALADEVA

ŚIVASTOTRĀVALĪ
OF
UTPALADEVA

Sanskrit Text with Introduction, English Translation and Glossary

N. K. KOTRU

MOTILAL BANARSIDASS
Delhi Varanasi Patna Madras

Head Office: Bungalow Road, Delhi 110 007
Branches: Chowk, Varanasi 221 001
Ashok Rajpath, Patna 800 004
6 Appar Swamy Koil Street, Mylapore,
Madras 600 004

First Edition: Delhi, 1985

ISBN: 0-89581-740-3

Printed in India by Shantilal Jain at Shri Jainendra Press,
A-45 Naraina, Phase I, New Delhi 110 028 and published by
Narendra Prakash Jain for Motilal Banarsidass, Delhi 110 007.

Dedicated with profound respects to the memory of my teacher, late Sri Ramji Handoo, whose scholarly guidance enabled me to understand the text in its proper perspective and whose encouragement has materialised in the present attempt.

CONTENTS

PREFACE

Of all sages and saints, who appeared in Kashmir from time to time, the name of Utpaladeva commands the greatest reverence, not only because he had keen philosophic insight or poetic genius but also because he had attained direct realization of the Supreme Reality. He was steeped in *Śiva* consciousness, and his sayings as such have been acclaimed as bearing the stamp of authority even by such teachers of eminence as the great Ācārya Abhinavagupta. Of all his works the present one enjoys greatest popularity among the masses as it forms a valuable treatise on *advaita bhakti* in the light of the *Śaiva* philosophy of Kashmir, and also because it is free from intellectual cobwebs. It throws a flood of light on the author's spiritual life containing a graphic account of his strivings, sufferings and experiences in the successive stages of spiritual evolution from the beginning to the attainment of the highest state of *Śiva*. It has been a source of inspiration to numberless people who have been anxious to solve the riddle of life and attain abiding bliss.

The work was first published in Chowkhamba Sanskrit Series Varanasi, many decades ago. A second edition came out in 1964 along with the commentary of Kṣemarāja as before with a word-for-word translation in Hindi by Sri Svami Laksman Joo of Srinagar, a *yogī* of high calibre and a traditional scholar of Kashmir *Śaivism*. The need for an English translation is self-evident as most people do not understand Sanskrit. The present translation is intended to help readers to understand the *ślokas* in original and follow the spirit that speaks through them. The introduction elucidates some hidden aspects of Śaivite philosophy in order to help in the understanding of the book. Copious notes have been added where necessary.

I have been helped in this task by my nephew, Sri Gobind Lal Shah, retired District Inspector of Schools, Srinagar and

Dr. B.K. Dembi, Reader Central Asian Studies, University of Kashmir, by going through the typescript and offering useful suggestions. I take this opportunity of expressing my indebtedness to them.

N.K. Kotru

INTRODUCTION

Utpaladeva is well known to students of Indian philosophy as the exponent of the Recognitive school of Kashmir *Śaivism* and the author of *Īśvara-pratyabhijñā-kārikā*, which together with the commentary of Abhinavagupta, known as *Vimarśinī* is a monumental work in the philosophic lore of the world. As admitted by the author in the very opening verse of the book, his exposition is not based on arid dialectics, but on his personal experience of the Ultimate Reality; it is nothing but a rational explanation of the truth of existence intuitionally apprehended and intellectually grasped after years of heroic struggle with forces of nature that thwart our vision of the Reality underlying the phenomenal world. Unfortunately, while his philosophy has caught the imagination of many a student, no attempt has so far been made to delve deep into his inner life and to explore the strong undercurrent of spirituality running beneath his rich intellectual endowments. His philosophy as such is the small visible portion of a colossal iceberg floating undiscovered underneath the surface. How he grappled with forces of nature in order to make his way to the dizzy heights of realization, that enabled him to solve the mystery of life and to take a panoramic view of his surroundings, is not fully appreciated. As a matter of fact, his spiritual life is as important as his philosophy, because it was on the bed-rock of his spirituality that he raised his wonderful structure of thought. Unless an attempt is made to study his inner life we shall not be able to do full justice to his person. The present study is an attempt in this direction, designed to bring to light a less known, but, nevertheless, an important facet of his many-splendoured personality. It can help us to understand the author as he really was.

No historical material has been vouchsafed to us about the author, and we are compelled to lean heavily on his own sayings, which serve the purpose of an auto-biography of his inner life. The picture that emerges must inevitably be of unimpeachable authenticity though lacking in biographic details. However, in regard to mahātmās it is the inner life that is of significance. Other details are of secondary importance.

About the Book

The present book, Śivastotrāvalī, is a collection of stray verses composed by the author at different periods, in different conditions, and discovered by his admirers in total disarray. They were collected by one Viśvāvarta and compiled into twenty *stotras* under the present name, and commented upon by Kṣemarāja, the author's great-grand-disciple. Of the twenty *stotras* only three bear the order given to them by the author himself, while the rest, which have come down to us in the recension of Viśvāvarta, hardly justify the name by any accepted canons of Sanskrit poetry. In fact, they are disconnected verses reflecting philosophical thoughts, emotional stresses, doubts and experiences of the author at various stages of his spiritual evolution. The mere fact that most of them are addressed to the Supreme Reality does not make them *stotras*. Nonetheless, we are indebted to Viśvāvarta for having given them a book form and to Kṣemarāja for his invaluable commentary.

The book is not the attempt of a philosophic genius to elaborate a thought system. Its value lies in the simple fact that it contains the spontaneous outpourings of a master mind set on the discovery of the truth of existence and its application to life on earth. The verses are free from intellectual embellishments, and retain the purity of the spirit that speaks through them. In fact, we can feel through them not only the author's consummate wisdom, but also his very heart beat and temper at different stages of his *sādhanā*.

India has always been a land of seers and thinkers who delved deep into the mysteries of existence and enriched us with the fruit of their investigations. But few of them have cared to leave behind them graphic accounts of their strivings, their difficulties and experiences at different stages of *sādhanā* in the way Utpaladeva has done. The book, therefore, is of great value to seekers as it throws valuable light on the path of spiritual progress—the risks involved and the gains to be harvested as a result of strenuous effort. It constitutes an authentic saga of one of the greatest spiritual adventures in the history of mankind. It is, however, essential to study the book as a whole, as in the absence of proper chronological arrangement it becomes extremely difficult to understand each verse in its proper context. It is like a beautiful image, broken into pieces, awaiting discerning fingers to place each one in its proper place so as to form a coherent whole.

The Turning Point

The path of spirituality is not open to all. "Among thousands of men", Says Lord Kṛṣṇa, "Scarce one striveth for perfection; of the successful strivers scarce one knoweth me in essence."[1] This path attracts only those thoughtful persons whose sense of disconsolateness with the life of senses is sufficiently developed and who are in quest of abiding peace and bliss. This feeling may be due to an inborn tendency or caused by some sort of a shock to one's personality; but in either case it is the consciousness of suffering coupled with the realization of one's limitations that shatters man's ego, and prompts him to probe into its causes. In his attempt to rid himself of pain and suffering man becomes aware of his insignificance as an individual, and looks forward to a higher power for help and guidance. But for pain and suffering man would not be conscious of his limitations and the need to overcome them. This consciousness is an essential pre-requisite for all spiritual life in the world.

It is evident from the author's own admission that at no time was he a stranger to the realm of spirituality. "At Thy own pleasure, O Lord, have I taken birth as Thy servant", Says he, "None else has a hand in this".[2] As such he was a born thinker and a devotee, one of those rare souls, who appear on the world scene with a mission and a message of love. He was horrified to see darkness, disharmony and suffering on all sides. Life was dominated by old age, disease and death, while the much coveted sense objects offered no happiness worth the

1. Bhagavadgītā VII. 3.
2. Verse 12/26.

name. Being extremely inquisitive, he sought an explanation for this sorry state of things, and strove to find lasting peace not only for himself but also for mankind as a whole. He was not satisfied with the life of senses, and therefore he wanted to probe into the mystery of life with a view to discover the source of lasting happiness. He felt extremely distressed, and gave vent to his feelings thus: "Ignorant am I, woe-stricken, scared by old age and other maladies. Being powerless, I have taken refuge in Thee. Deign, O Lord, that I may ere long attain the highest of all states past the path of pain."[1] Again, "Endless is the cycle of birth and death; the slender frame gets withered by diseases sharp and diverse. Sense pleasures I did not enjoy. What little happiness I came by on occasions did not endure. Thus, born in vain, grant, O Lord, that Thy devotee, with head illumined by the touch of the feet of the crescent-bedecked Lord here and now attains sublime and lasting wealth."[2]

Since the beginning of life man has never felt satisfied with his environments. Deep down in his heart he has felt a sense of disconsolateness and a subtle urge to go beyond the phenomenal existence, and probe into the mysteries of life and the universe around. The universe with all its wonderful laws does not explain itself, while the intellect cannot operate beyond a fixed point or know what is beyond itself. After continuous struggle it comes to realize its helplessness and the fact that it is animated by a power far beyond its ken. Truth is something beyond the reach of mind and speech, and the realization of this fact accounts for the genesis of faith and devotion, which alone are capable of satisfying the basic urge of the human soul.

Utpaladeva set himself to the Herculean task of exploring the upper reaches of the stream of consciousness which animated the mind and the senses in its course downwards. He broke new ground and strove hard to delve into the depths of his own being which is no other than the universal self. Eventually he found himself transported into ethereal regions where the mind or the intellect has no access. He was innocent yet earnest in his quest, and laid bare before the Lord all that he thought and

1. Verse 11/8.
2. Verse 15/19.

felt as a true aspirant. With the Lord Standing manifestly in his form of supreme light, he wondered why realization did not come to him without effort. When everything owed its birth and sustenance to the Lord, why was the world smouldering within? "Suffocating within the egg-shell of the world, formed of attachment etc. he longed to grow wings and become a denizen of the heavens."[1] These and similar musings gave rise to highest form of devotion, unknown before, and in due time answered his questions and set all doubts at rest.

Rise of Advaita Śaivism

This was the starting point of a great quest—an attempt to explore the inmost depths of consciousness and to master the forces that make life narrow and crippled. Utpaladeva was full of resolution, and set out on his adventure under the able guidance of his guru, the *siddha* Somānanda, whose doctrine of Recognition he was later commissioned to propagate so ably in his life.

The various creeds and systems of thought prevalent at the time did not appeal to him and he rejected them one by one as dry intellectual exercises having no value in practice. Buddhism did not accept the authority of *Vedas*, *Āgamas* or any other *pramāṇas* except one's own intellect. Buddha exhorted his followers to be a light unto themselves and not to recognize any outside authority including that of Buddha himself. Though his own *sambodhi* was based on intuition, what he gave his followers was based on cold reason. This gave rise to numberless schools of thought, whose pure intellectualism ran counter to the author's basic approach.

The valley of Kashmir, like the rest of India, remained under Buddhist influence upto the eighth century of the Christian Era, when Vasugupta appeared on the scene and changed the whole current of religious thought. He propagated the *Śiva Sūtras*, revealed to him by *Śiva* Himself as engraved on a big stone still identified as *Śaṅkara Pala* at the eastern foot of the Mahādeva mountain, a few miles away from Harwan reservoir in Srinagar. They contained the essence of *Śaivāgamas*, the authoritative scriptures of *Advaita Śaivism*, and with these he was able to

1. Verse 7/4.

counter the nihilistic teachings of Buddhism, which did not recognize the existence either of a permanent subject or a supreme being known as God. Vasugupta popularized the worship of *Śiva* as the ultimate Reality accessible within one's own self.

Buddhism based its teachings on pure rationalism which did not carry emotional appeal apart from the personality of its founder. As time wore on, it branched off into numberless creeds whose followers engaged themselves in wordy duels without being able to satisfy the mass mind. These intellectual acrobats failed to meet the natural urge of the human soul, and people, therefore, hailed the new movement as the easiest way to salvation, and derived satisfaction from it. It was about the same time as the great Śaṅkarācārya launched his vigorous campaign in the south and popularized the cult of *bhakti*. He propounded the philosophy of *Advaita Vedānta*, and with his powerful logic defeated Buddhist scholars everywhere during his sweeping tour of the country. He was essentially a great *bhakta* and a *tantric* worshipper, whose devotional songs especially his *Saundarya Laharī*, are acclaimed as masterpieces in Sanskrit literature. He composed hymns in praise of almost all gods and goddesses in the Hindu pantheon. They appealed to the mass mind everywhere, and popularized the cult of *bhakti* giving birth to a number of saints from all classes of the society. The life and teachings of these saints fired the imagination of people throughout the country, and added new vigour to the old religion, which, though lying low for about twelve centuries of Buddhist domination, was very much alive. In fact, it was a movement of renaissance of the old religion.

In Kashmir the work of Vasugupta was continued by other teachers, and completed by Utpaladeva and his illustrious follower, the great Abhinavagupta. Utpaladeva was full of compassion for suffering humanity, and after attaining *siddhi* wrote his famous *Pratyabhijñā-Kārikā* in order to help his fellow beings to attain the highest end of life. He proved the existence of a permanent subject as identical with *Maheśvara*, and put final seal on the efforts of his predecessors not only through his own power of reasoning but also by his personal example of spiritual attainments. Like Paramahaṁsa Ramakrishna in our own times, he was steeped in God consciousness, and demonstrated in his own person how man could attain realization by *bhakti* without arduous penances or *yogic* practices. He checked the tidal wave of nihilism in the same way as the Ramakrishna-Vivekananda axis counter-influenced the growing materialistic wave from the West during recent times. Being unlettered, the Paramahaṁsa relied on his able disciple for the propagation of his mission, while Utpaladeva possessed all the qualities of the master and the disciple in one. He was born at a propitious time when there was intellectual chaos and spiritual degeneration in the country. By his towering personality he was able to rehabilitate the faith of the people in the tenets of *Śaivism*, which had received a set-back during the long period of Buddhist domination. While Śaṅkara compromised with some of the teachings and institutions of Buddhism, it was in Kashmir that the latter received its death blow.

This movement declared that all men were equal, and high birth was no qualification for salvation. God alone is superior, and he is accessible to all alike when invoked with sincere devotion. Devotees of the Lord, though of humble birth, are as much adorable as God Himself, while those devoid of God's love, though claiming high birth, are to be shunned as impure. Love of God is the only purifier of the body and the mind. Says the author, "O Lord, the fountain-head of beauty as Thou art, at Thy touch everything becomes invaluable, be that a jewel or a piece of straw."[1] God's grace knows no bounds, and this makes all creatures, including lower animals, fit for salvation. Those who are devoid of God's love are lowly and despicable despite high birth. Referring to such persons the author says, "Those persons, O Lord, whose hearts are not immersed in the joy of Thy love, are heartless indeed. They are worthy of contempt."[2]

This movement ushered in an era of peace throughout the country by bringing together people of all denominations. Members of all classes sat together and held spiritual discourses bringing comfort to many a parched soul. The impact of this

1. Verse 16/26.
2. Verse 3/7.

moment was felt even outside the Hindu fold. A number of Muslim saints joined their voices with their counterparts in Hindu society, and created a spiritual fellowship. The influence of these saints is still visible in the contemporary literature. The occasional reference to wine and sweetheart in the present book is an unmistakable evidence of the imprint of the *Sufi* Cult.

The path propounded herein is based on the doctrine of *Advaita* as declared in monistic *Śaivāgamas.* It is a synthesis of all the three paths of *jñāna*, *karma* and *bhakti*, which are complementary to each other and not independent means to the realization of the goal of life. Human nature has three main aspects—intellectual, emotional and conational, and in order to attain full-blooded realization of the Divine, all one's faculties must be thrown into the effort. It is not enough to dedicate to it merely our intellects or emotions or merely actions because in that case the gain will be partial and not integral. Our intellect must be directed towards knowing Him, our emotional nature towards loving and all actions towards serving Him. Great souls are those who combine in their lives a heart imbued with infinite love and an intellect illumined with the knowledge of God. They are not content with partial gains. Spiritual development must be all-round and not lop-sided. The goal is devotion to the Supreme Being who combines in Himself the mobile and the immobile, to love Him, to know Him fully and to enter into His being. Wisdom, devotion and work go together.

The author takes into account both the transcendental and the immanent aspects of Reality and does not find any sharp difference between the two ends of existence. The world of consciousness and that of senses are inseparably connected, and in order to make life free and unfettered, it is essential to master both. Spirituality is not something far removed from the demands of daily life, and does not mean escapism or otherworldliness. The life of utter renunciation is not incompatible with worldly life, which has its own place in the scheme of things. *Śaiva* teachers did not subscribe to the doctrine of *sannyāsa* as an institution. Escapism is no substitute for spirituality. It is not necessary to throw away the world, and to kill the senses or entirely inhibit their legitimate activities, nor is it necessary to spend one's whole time in meditation. In that case one gets into the habit of living in an inner world entirely losing contact with external realities. This will bring in one-sided, inharmonious movement, and may lead to disturbance of balance. To do both meditation and work and dedicate both to the Lord is the best course for an aspirant. The author does not recognize any contradiction between worldly acts and spiritual life. All acts become sacred in the hands of a spiritual man, while sacred acts may be dragged down to a vulgar level by a man of materialistic outlook. With the dawn of wisdom all acts of man are transmuted into worship of the Lord. It was with this in view that Lord Kṛṣṇa exhorted Arjuna to remember Him and also fight. The author prayed, "Like common folk, O Lord, let me have increased infatuation for sense objects. Only would I behold them as Thy being having lost all sense of differentiation."[1] Again says he, "Let these senses of mine delightfully fall on their respective objects. Yet not for a moment may I, O Lord, run the slightest risk of parting with the bliss of harmony with Thee."[2] The aim is to sublimate life and remain in constant awareness of the self while performing all acts of daily life.

The universe with its smooth and orderly working points unerringly to a skilled hand. The whole order of creation follows a meticulous plan, and is too meaningful to be dismissed as an error. Everything here has a divine purpose, and every individual a part to play. In this colossal organism each part moves according to a set plan, harmoniously playing the role assigned to it by a master designer. "This world," says Sri Aurobindo, "was not built with the bricks of chance; a conscious power has drawn the plan of life, and there is meaning in every curve and line." Individual life is not cut off from the whole, and must not be viewed in isolation. It is governed by a grand law that guides its course on earth. The whole creation is the Lord's play. A devotee considers himself as an instrument in the hands of the Divine, and plays his role as a willing partner in the divine *līlā*. It is not for man to move away from the scheme of things. Says the author, "Not a thought arises that does not constitute Thy will. All actions—meritorious or otherwise—are being

1. Verse 8/3.
2. Verse 8/5.

performed by the Lord Himself. Thus abiding in Thee, I live unfettered walking the earth with nothing to frustrate the festival of worshipping Thy stainless feet."[1] Every moment the devotee finds the guiding hand of the Supreme, and beholds His will as directing all events in the world. In all trials and tribulations he sees the Lord's finger at work, and submits unconditionally to it.

This system does not recognize any essential difference between the individual self, technically called the *paśu* and the Universal Self, the *Pati*. Spirituality is an attempt on the part of the *paśu* to break the shackles of *Māyā* and rise into the free and unfettered state of the *Pati*, or in the author's own words, to break through the egg-shell of the world formed of attachment and aversion and to grow wings so as to be able to become a denizen of the limitless space of consciousness. Man is potentially divine. Every aspect of the Divinity has got its counterpart in man, and as such one can reach the Divinity by sublimating these aspects in oneself. *Bhakti* is the natural way to achieve this end. The fact that it starts with a feeling of duality does not tarnish its character as it consummates in total oneness with the object of worship. Says the author, "Eliminating from Thy worship the plaintive element of devotion, implying duality, the chosen few, O Lord, enjoy Thy immaculate form of immortality."[2]

SPIRITUAL AWAKENING: ITS PRE-CONDITION

The basic problem for man in the world is not the attainment of liberation, but an earnestness to rise above the narrow life of the senses and live a free and unfettered life of the spirit. Spiritual endeavour, like all other undertakings, demands congenial atmosphere for its growth and consummation. Spirituality, they say, is a contagion, which can be caught and not taught. This is provided by the association of good and godly persons, who have either realized their identity or have attained an advanced stage in the path. The contact of these blessed souls inspires spiritual awakening among thoughtless people too much engros-

1. Verse 12/22.
2. Verse 16/13.

sed in worldly life, besides helping those who are already on the way to spiritual goal. *Satsaṅga* has been declared by all the *śāstras* as the first step in sādhanā, and an unmistakable sign of divine grace, as it provides suitable environment for spiritual growth. The company of holy persons helps to keep the mind free from evil tendencies giving rise to single-minded devotion. All vanities are dissolved, and the mind is purged of all impurities making it possible to reflect the light of knowledge. *Mahātmās* help mankind by their sayings, their movements and thought currents. Their mere presence is able to bring solace to afflicted souls. "Like *Śiva* flowers they lend fragrance to those living nearby possessing perverse tendencies."[1] We have got living examples of agnostics having turned saints by the mere contact of holy persons given to service of love. Devotees always seek the company of like-minded persons, and together spend their time in spiritual discourses, singing praises of the Lord and His devotees. The author says that the Lord invariably blesses such assemblies by His presence.

Bhakti: its significance

When man becomes conscious of his limitations the urge for a life of freedom becomes irresistible. This urge is the author's *bhakti*. It is the master key to liberation and all that it implies. According to the author what goes by the name of *mukti* is but the consummation of *bhakti*. Super-conscious experience, he says, appears before a devotee as a pillar of rubbing stone when love-itch gains intensity, or as a lake of cool and sweet water when one becomes athirst for realization. It is the fountain-head of all that is of value and a panacea for all ills. Says the author, "What are spoken of as the fruit of *siddhis* starting with *aṇimā* and others and ending in liberation are simply inherent in the creeper of love that has attained ripeness."[2] Again, "When a pitcher full of milk is in hand vain is the quest for curds."[3] *Bhakti* is its own reward and not means to an end.

The philosophy of love as reflected in the book is not one

1. Verse 15/16.
2. Verse 1/25.
3. Verse 15/12.

that envisages worship of a personal god as something separate from our being, nor does it point out a path to which we are total strangers. It simply brings to light a natural process constantly at work within our very being. What is demanded is proper understanding of a simple truth, and living in constant awareness of it. Says the author, "Thou art the self of all, and all are lovers of the self. Thus attains excellence the man who knows Thy love as inhering in all."[1] Love of self is the supreme urge of the individual common to all. It is for the sake of the self that one loves all else. Bliss is the very nature of the self, and though caught in the labyrinth of *Māyā* and somehow reduced to a state of helplessness, the individual strives, imperceptibly though, to regain his pristine state and to re-discover himself. The quest for happiness is as old as life itself. All acts of the individual are prompted by this natural urge in an unconscious effort to regain the lost treasure. Consciously or unconsciously, everyone loves the divinity of the self, and it is the ignorance of this simple truth that makes a man run after sense objects in search of happiness. The real fount of joy lies within the depths of our own being, and is a natural object of love and worship. "The golden oriole is ever warbling in the mountain thicket of the body"[2] and all that a devotee has to do is to tune his ears to its melody. This cultivates self-awareness without any discipline, tortuous practices or meaningless rituals, and helps one to get merged into the bliss of one's own being.

Bhakti is the path of the heart and consists in blending all sorts of emotions into a supreme feeling of identity with the object of love. It is a natural way of bringing about union of the individual self with the Universal Self. All that is required is cultivating understanding and purging the mind of all materialistic tendencies. All other disciplines, being material in nature and based on ignorance, are unilluminative and not conducive to light. The author did not recognize any other means for realization. Says he, "Neither *yoga* nor austerities, nor any other system of worship is recommended. In this cult of *Śiva*, which recognizes no material means, *bhakti* alone is

1. Verse 2/7.
2. Verse 14/19.

eulogized."[1] The other paths recommended by the *Śāstras* are only capable of giving partial satisfaction corresponding to physical, intellectual and vital urges of man. They are termed as material means, falling within the domain of *Māyā*, the principle of obscuration. *Jñāna* without *bhakti* is tasteless, tending to boost the ego sense while *bhakti* sweetens life. The author rejects *yogic* practices in strongest terms as of little spiritual value by themselves. They do not hold the key to salvation. The awakening of *kuṇḍalinī* may bring all sorts of *siddhis*, but the basic urge of the human soul can only be satisfied by *bhakti*. All other paths are contributory and of secondary importance. Says the author, "Lord, that Thou art attainable in a particular stage or a particular place by *yoga* is sheer humbug. Else, how art Thou visible to lovers in all states ?"[2]

Bhakti does not call for a specific ritual or a technique of worship. What is required is constant remembrance of the Lord and chanting His name. The devotee overflows with the thought, and pants for it with all his heart. The mind is enchanted by the sweet music of the name, and filled with a strange joy equal to the joy of all sense pleasures put together and more. Whenever the mind goes astray, it can be steadied by the sweet music of the name. To attain concentration of mind there is no practice easier or more potent than repetition of the divine name. Other forms of *sādhanā* tend to boost egotism, while the name helps to dissolve it. When the mind is stilled by the practice of the name, one attains a state of self-awareness and realizes one's identity with the eternal truth transcending relative existence. In the beginning it requires effort to maintain this awareness, but by constant practice one becomes established in this blessed state of consciousness, and comes to realize that the lover and the loved are one. In the silent retreats of the heart the devotee experiences the rapture of the music of the divine name. The author extols the name every now and then, and says, "They have secured instant release from the tentacles of pain—endless and invincible—those whose speech ever resounds with the sound *Śiva*."[3] Again, "He alone

1. Verse 1/18.
2. Verse 1/16.
3. Verse 3/13.

is exalted whose speech is adorned with the name of *Maheśvara*"[1] It is said that *Śiva* is bodily present where His name is being sung.

Love knows no limitations of time or place. It is the true self of all, bliss absolute. When it gains momentum *vṛttis* of the mind are stilled without any effort. The lover experiences divine presence within and without, and feels the joy of liberation here itself. He is not deluded by the relation of the subject and the object. Experiences of pleasure and pain do not shake him, but rather heighten his conviction. In fact, the lover enters the kingdom of God and enjoys the bliss of fulfilment. At the very moment love of God dawns within him. Says the author, "Great Lord, the moment I set foot on Thy path at Thy own bidding, all blessedness dawned on me there and then. What else may I seek of Thee?"[2]

Lovers have nothing to stand in their way. They live like common folk, but are alert within. They live in the world, but do not belong to it. To them the world is a swimming pool and not a prison house. They have no wants and nothing to chain them. "Adoration to the blessed souls, who, going nowhere and renouncing nothing, yet behold all this as Thy blest light."[3] "They mock at the Lord of creation as one having become enslaved by bonds of authority". Nothing can frustrate their realization of divine presence.

Devotion is not mere emotional effervescence, but the recognition of the divine nature of all things and beings. The essential qualification of a devotee is to see and worship the Lord abiding in all creatures. An ethical life based on self-discipline, benevolence and charity is an essential requirement for progress in the spiritual field. The quality of devotion depends on the nature of a devotee. Devotees have been classified into three categories according to their nature: sāttvika, rājasika and tāmasika. Of these a devotee who sees and worships the Lord everywhere and in all creatures belongs to the highest class. Those who neglect the needs and sufferings of fellow beings can at best be

1. Verse 10/23.
2. Verse 4/21.
3. Verse 20/10.

devotees of the ordinary class. Devotion devoid of right conduct effectively blocks spiritual progress. *Bhakti* connotes desirelessness and self-surrender. It is immaculate and spontaneous, not motivated. Desire is the root cause of bondage. Even the desire for liberation as a means of escape from the hardships of life is an impediment in spiritual life. According to the teachings of *Śaivism* such persons are deluded by *Māyā* utilizing just their desire for liberation. A man of wisdom seeks nothing apart from the love of God, and is content with his lot. He considers himself as a channel for the flow of God's will, and moves harmoniously with the scheme of things. Devotion is its own reward, an end in itself. Says the author, "To the inebriates of love there is, O Lord, not the least craving for happiness as a means to the overcoming of suffering. In the audience of the Heart Captivator, even the supplication for liberation is not remembered."[1]

When devotion gets intensified, attachment for sense objects is lost along with the sense of duality. The ego and the mind-stuff are dissolved, and the worshipper is transformed into the very object of worship. The author says, "To great ones, O Lord of immortals, though the object of worship, Thou constantly stayeth as the worshipper."[2] Kabir has beautifully expressed the same experience : "So long as I-ness existed, the teacher could not enter; with the parting of I-ness the teacher stepped in. For the lane of love is very narrow, two it cannot contain."[3] When devotion reaches its climax no trace of duality remains. The devotee feels himself as the very object of worship. When Paramahaṁsa Ramakrishna was absorbed in the worship of the Divine Mother, he often placed flowers on his own head. It is said that *Śrī Rādhā* felt the pangs of separation from her beloved so acutely that she was metamorphosed into Kṛṣṇa and then began to pine for Rādhā. Tears flowed from her eyes, and her voice faltered as she cried Rādhā, Rādhā, Rādhā, and as a result she again became Rādhā. Such is the peculiarity of love.

1. Verse 18/15.
2. Verse 4/25.
3. Bankey Behary: *Sufis, Mystics and Yogis of India*, pp. 230 (Bharatiya Vidya Bhavan Publication).

Utpaladeva believed that salvation was possible by no other means than *bhakti* combined with divine grace. *Bhakti* is the sovereign remedy whose natural corollary is what goes by the name of *mukti*. It is the culmination of both *jñāna* and *yoga*. The two are simply means to *bhakti*, the master key to the discovery of the Ultimate Reality lying beyond the faculty of reason. Knowledge without *bhakti* is inconsequential and sterile, not able to satisfy the basic urge of the human soul. One must go beyond the mind and the intellect and experience the Divine with one's whole being. "Devoid of the experience of love," Says the author, "Knowledge, however advanced, appears to me as sour as a ferment."[1] *Parā bhakti* is the end of knowledge, and the only means to complete realization and entrance into the being of the Lord. Lord Kṛṣṇa declares in the Gītā, "At the close of many a birth, the man of realization worships Me, realizing that 'all this is *Vāsudeva*.' "[2] Discovery of the Supreme is a super-conscious experience and not philosophic speculation. Unlike the one to be acquired from books, this unwritten knowledge is beautifully extolled by the author thus: "On the infinite tablet of unitive experience, brimming over with immortal freedom, I bow, O Lord, to that philosophy of Thine which knows no script."[3] All that is required to achieve the goal of unitive experience is intelligent devotion and earnestness of effort. When one is established in this consciousness one is no longer held captive by the world of senses. One beholds the Lord everywhere and enjoys divine presence in all states of existence. To the devotee the whole creation recites the tale of the Lord, and he enjoys the bliss of liberation in day-to-day life. Pleasure and pain do not disturb the even flow of his life. He sees light and beauty where there was darkness before. The author extols such great and rare souls, and says, "Most exalted are those world honoured votaries of Thine, O Lord of the universe, to whom this very ocean of the world constitutes a vast swimming pool."[4] In this grand experience bondage and liberation lose their

1. Verse 1/11.
2. Bhagavadgītā 7/19.
3. Verse 2/27.
4. Verse 3/15.

meaning. This cult, which combines in itself both knowledge and devotion is variously spoken of by the author as the path of *Śiva*, *Śaṅkara* or *Maheśvara*, and is summarized by him as under:—

Where miseries become pleasure,
Where poison turns into nectar,
Where the world itself is transmuted into liberation—
That is the path of *Śaṅkara*.[1]

We come close to God wherever there is beauty, love and truth. God reveals Himself in the beauties of nature, nobility of character, works of art and highest achievements of the mind. Recounting His *vibhūtis* Lord Kṛṣṇa tells Arjuna, "Whatsoever is glorious, good, beautiful and mighty, understand that to have sprung from a part of my splendour."[2] Commenting on this Dr. Radhakrishnan says, "While all things are supported by God, things of beauty and splendour reveal Him more than others. Every deed of heroism, every life of sacrifice, every work of genius, is a revelation of the Divine."

Man is free to worship God in His formless state. But this is hard to follow. It is not easy to set the mind on the formless. The author himself seems to have started his spiritual life with the worship of *Śiva* in His personal form as is evident from a number of stanzas in the book itself. This must have been of immense help in his struggle to concentrate on the formless and to dive deep into the unfathomable depths of consciousness. "The difficulties of those intent on the formless are greater,"[3] says the Lord in the Bhagavadgītā. A lover on the other hand beholds the Lord in all His manifestations, and worships even blades of grass as *Śiva*. He admires the Lord in all His manifestations, sings of His glories and loves Him. "The great distinctive feature of lovers, not given to *pratyāhāra* and other practices, as against *yogīs*, is that they remain poised even in *vyutthāna*." They despise nothing and need not restrain their

1. Verse 20/12.
2. Bhagavadgītā 10.41.
3. Ibid 12.5.

senses from their legitimate objects, as nothing is alien to them. They respond joyously to beauty in life and the nature around. "People given to vanity do not cognize the essential nature of things, though full of beauty on proper investigation."[1] Lovers belong to a different category with a different outlook. "Wherefore may not the mind pursue all objects of desire as Thyself ? Thus, it will not lose its nature and my highest dream will also be realized."[2] Again says the author, "Dwelling in the ocean of supreme immortality, with the mind immersed in the mere act of worshipping Thee, let me perform all human operations, all the same imbibing something ineffable."[3]

Lovers adore the Lord in all His manifestations, in all phenomena of nature, the starry firmament, moonlit nights, flora and fauna, snowy peaks and rippling lakes. They love the sweet music of murmuring brooks and rustling leaves as singing the glory of the Lord, and attain realization with eyes wide open. To them the whole of creation reflects the glory of the Lord. Says the author, "He who beholds all this objectivity as Thy undifferentiated form, fills the whole universe with his own self. To such an ever happy soul whence the fear ?"[4] Again, "Through the mouths of all his senses he drinks of the wine of worship in brimful cups of all objects and gets maddened."[5]

The lover does not disregard his body as a prison house, but as a temple for the worship of the Lord. The body must be pure and strong so as to be able to bear the shock of *samādhi*. A weak and impure body is an obstacle in the path of spirituality.

Bhakti pre-supposes superiority of the object of worship, and a feeling of surrender on the part of the devotee. Man is no doubt divine in essence, but in the absence of this awareness the mere chanting of *Śivo'ham* is of no consequence. Says the author, "I am the Lord; I, the luminous; I am the omniscient and graceful I am. Who on earth is the like of me ?—such a feeling of

1. Verse 18/3.
2. Verse 12/20.
3. Verse 18/13.
4. Verse 13/16.
5. Verse 13/8.

dignity behoves none but Thy devotees."[1] Paramahaṁsa Ramakrishna expresses the same view when he says, "What is the good of repeating the word *Śivo'ham* ? It is only when one, by perfect meditation on the Lord in the temple of one's own heart, has lost all idea of the self, and realized the Lord *Śiva* within, that one is entitled to utter the sacred word. What good can the mere repetition of the formula do without the realization ? So long as the state of realization is not reached, it is better to regard the Lord as the master and oneself as His humble servant." The author never called himself *Śiva*, but proclaimed himself as *Śivadāsaḥ*. He regarded *Śiva* as the master, and dedicated his body, mind and speech exclusively to Him. This feeling of humility persisted even after his self-recognition, which he simply called *dāsyam*. He remained the very picture of humility both before and after attaining *siddhi*. Devotees do not seek merger into the featureless *Brahman*, but prefer to remain face to face with the Lord enjoying divine presence. It is a grand experience known only to a chosen few. Says the author, "What happiness is there that is not attainable by Śiva's servant—one dwelling in oneness with Śiva ?"[2] A devotee prefers the status of a servant in relation to his Lord even in the height of spiritual perfection.

MIND : ITS NATURE AND CONTROL

The greatest impediment in spiritual life is an impure mind, the storehouse of all *vāsanās* that bind a man to the life of senses. It is like a volcano that produces powerful thought waves. It is mysterious in nature, extremely fast moving, calling for heroic effort to keep it under restraint. It is the connecting link between the world of senses and that of consciousness, and is, therefore, responsible for both bondage and liberation. Being possessed of contradictory tastes, it hankers after sense objects in worldly life and also enjoys the bliss of unitive experience in *samādhi*. It is capable of yielding wonderful results when concentrated on any object. There is no limit to its powers which can be harnessed to one's well-being or downfall. The

1. Verse 13/4.
2. Verse 10/25.

author says that it is the seed of all suffering in the world, yet capable of yielding the supreme fruit of liberation when saturated with devotion. As a matter of fact, the very aim of *sādhanā* is to tame the mind and purge it of all impure tendencies so as to be able to reflect the light of the true self within and get liquidated in the process. The senses have been likened to thieves on the spiritual path demanding strict vigil on the part of a seeker.

It is not an easy job to curb the mind, but it can be steadied by practice of meditation and dispassion. If, however, one is not able to concentrate on the inner self, one need not get disheartened. One is free to concentrate on anything external or internal as everything is *Śiva*. Realization can emanate out of things dearest to one's heart provided they are viewed in the right perspective without personal attachment. Rāmatīrtha realized God in the beauties of the Himālayas, and in the height of ecstasy actually lost his body in the Gaṅgā. Aurobindo worshipped India as the Divine Mother, and started *sādhanā* for redeeming her honour. Consequently, his first experience of God came to him in Alipore Jail.

Restraint of mind by force is not of much avail unless it comes across something more absorbing. It is only the bliss of devotion that can wean it away from sense objects and make it dispassionate. When the bliss of the higher self is experienced, sense-pleasures will easily lose their hold on the *sādhaka*. Lord Kṛṣṇa declares in the Gītā, "The objects of sense but not the relish thereof turn away from an abstemious dweller in the body, and even that turneth away when the Supreme is seen."[1] *Bhakti* is the easiest way of taming the mind. Even a moment's experience of the joy of higher consciousness is able to still the mind and to change the very course of a seeker's life. Says the author, "Those who are blessed with just a trail of the aroma of Thy lotus feet, to them all objects of enjoyment, coveted even by gods, appear stinking."[2]

The mind, according to this system, is nothing but consciousness having subjected itself to a condition of limitation through

1. Bhagavadgītā 2.59.
2. Verse 11/6.

its native power of freedom. In fact, it is a mere derivative of the spirit, and has no existence apart from it. As such, it is possible to make the mind disappear and revert to the state of the spirit from which it is derived. It functions in two ways. When limitation dominates it falls down into the state of *paśu*, but when consciousness prevails as a result of earnest effort, subordinating limitation, it enters the sphere of the pure path (*śuddhādhva*) ascending step by step to the state of *Śiva* when it undergoes total transformation.

The status of realized beings varies in proportion to the extent to which they have been able to control the mind. Those who have fewer *vāsanās* do not require much effort to attain the highest end of life, while those whose minds are crowded with them, attain their goal in the course of several births. Those of the *jñānīs* who, for want of requisite effort, have still some *vāsanās* left in them are known as *samanaskas* and their state as *samanā*. When the mind is free from agitation, it is called *unmanā* (supra-mental state). The former belong to the lower class as they are still affected by pleasure and pain, and are still under the influence of *prārabdha*. *Jñānīs* of the latter class are *jīvanmuktas* and they belong to the highest class. They are able to stay in any plane of consciousness without losing their identity.

There are some gifted souls blessed with a sharp memory, who have acquired a pure mind free from *vāsanās* either as a result of good deeds performed in previous births or due to single-minded devotion to God. They can attain the highest goal all of a sudden as if by accident like a fruit fallen from above without any discipline such as *dhyāna* or *samādhi*. A mere talk of God is enough to transport them into the highest plane of spiritual experience. King Janaka of old is quoted as an instance. The author seems to have found it difficult to reconcile himself to the why and how of phenomenal events of this type taking place in the spiritual world. As such, he addressed himself to the Lord and said, "By what scheme of Thine does this love for Thee ripen in Thy devotees, so that a mere mention or a reminder in the state of separation begets the joy of a tryst ?"[1]

1. Verse 4/12.

It is equally clear that he himself did have some such experience which impelled him to say, "Let this zest of devotion, unknown before, reach its climax the same way as it emanated in me."[1] In course of time he got fully reconciled to unusual events of this type in the case of those who have purged their minds of all impurities.

Worship Defined

The worship so frequently mentioned in the book is not conventional worship conducted through the body using flowers and other things for the propitiation of a particular deity. Real worship is that in which the ego along with the whole of mind-stuff are consecrated as offerings to the Divinity within the temple of the heart. In this processs the mind and the intellect are blended into a constant current flowing into the depths of consciousness. The *sādhaka* loses separate existence and assumes a new identity with the Divine. The worshipper transcends the limited self and experiences the light and bliss of higher consciousness. The distinction between the worshipper and the worshipped is lost, and the two are rolled into one. The author goes so far as to say that the Divinity itself stays as the worshipper. There is no object of knowledge. The light of consciousness reigns supreme. There is extreme beauty that captivates the worshipper's heart. The author defines worship as "the flow of the bliss of union with the Lord." According to *Śrī Vijñāna Bhairava*, worship is not the setting of the heart on the object of worship with the aid of flowers and others, but is getting lost in the infinite void of consciousness. No regulations are prescribed and no formalities called for. The worshipper experiences a bliss that surpasses imagination. It is a matter of personal experience which no one has been able to translate into human language. Worldly joys dwindle into insignificance. Says the author, "Methinks, not an iota of the wealth of happiness is experienced by man until the grand festival of imbibing the nectar of Thy worship is attained."[2] He asserts that the over-

1. Verse 16/5.
2. Verse 17/21.

lordship of the three worlds holds no charm for one who has had a moment's experience of the sublime bliss. All his life gets imbued with the joy of this experience. The author tries his best to give us an inkling of this state, and exclaims, "Oh, exalted is this supreme festival of worship, ineffable and sweet, as an outcome of which even tears yield boundless joy of immortality."[1] He calls it Śiva's night as the world of relativity fades into oblivion while the devotee remains drowned in an ocean of bliss. All notions of time and space are lost, and the worhipper is one with Śiva.

Every now and then we come across passages in the book containing the author's invocation to the lotus feet of the Lord. These do not indicate worship of a personal God, though such worship is not decried by him. According to the commentator, the two feet represent the Lord's *Śaktis* of *jñāna* and *kriyā*, which are of great significance to *sādhakas*. *Mokṣa* according to this system is not mere dispelling of ignorance, but also full manifestation of the inherent potentialities of the self in the wake of realization. When a devotee enters the pure path, he becomes master of all *śaktis*, and acquires the powers of omniscience and omnipotence. He is no longer held captive by lower nature.

The experience of higher consciousness is known as *samādhi* or *samāveśa*. It is an advanced state of contemplation, and implies a thought-free mind. It is different from *suṣupti* in which the mind and senses become quiescent, and are enveloped in darkness. In *samāveśa*, on the other hand, the mind is fully awake, but being without thought it enjoys the bliss of *suṣupti*, and is, therefore, described by some as *suṣupti* in *jāgrata*. It is known as *turīyā*, the fourth, which is the substratum of all other states of consciousness. In the beginning the strain of the mind is felt in a subtle form, and is, therefore, called *savikalpa samādhi*. It is attended with effort in order to curb mental disturbances. Then there is the higher state known as *nirvikalpa samādhi* in which the mind is totally quiescent and the experience effortless. This is the state of *turīyātīta* or the

1. Verse 17/1.

one beyond the fourth, the state of *Parama Śiva*. The mind gets dissolved in the bliss of higher consciousness.

At first, the experience of *samādhi* comes like a flash of lightning causing nervous excitement and a rude shock to the body. One finds it difficult to withstand the brilliance of this beatific vision. The physical frame gets stiffened, the hair stands on end, the face flushes with laughter, while tears of joy roll down the cheeks. The body becomes practically dead to the world, while the devotee remains drowned in bliss. Though short-lived, it holds within a future promise, and creates confidence in the *sādhaka*. It is beyond the capacity of one to remain in this condition for long unless one has worked oneself up to that stage of evolution. The duration of samādhi, therefore, varies in the case of different *sādhakas*, and may last till an inner voice throws them back into the shores of limited existence. Initially, the strain caused to the body is great, but by constant practice it becomes a natural state of one's being. This experience is not a thing to be enjoyed occasionally, but to be lived in constant awareness in all conditions and all states of consciousness. An aspirant must not become complacent after having occasional flashes of higher consciousness, but must continue the effort till it becomes a permanent possession. Says the author, "This sovereign remedy of Thy love, the remover of the distress of birth and death, demands protecting, fostering and respect."[1] Any slackness in the effort is fraught with the gravest risks, and may let loose all the forces of lower nature that afflict a common man. As a matter of fact, it is the starting point of the real struggle between the two worlds, and demands super-human effort to carry it to a successful end. Again says the author, "Even for a moment shall I not be a fit receptacle for Thy vision, if I do not ceaselessly imbibe with ardent faith the bliss of oneness with Thee."[2]

There are lower forms of *samādhi* experienced by all in day to day life. They are induced by the impact of external stimuli on the mind making it one-pointed without effort, and thus bringing one nearer the state of realization. These are the

1. Verse 15/10.
2. Verse 4/18.

states of extreme anger, grief, exultation, bewilderment, fright and the like, such as when one feels enraptured at the sudden sight of some person or thing earnestly longed for but given up in despair, when one is confronted with utmost danger or when one hears of the sudden death of someone extremely dear. There are also intervals of *samādhi* between the waking, dream and deep sleep states, which are of extremely short duration, and people in ignorance do not detect them. They are known as momentary *samādhis*, and, as a rule, pass unnoticed by common man. In absence of proper knowledge they are not able to dispel ignorance or grant liberation. Though of no significance to common man, they are of great help to *yogīs* as stepping stones in their effort to realize the true self within. They seize upon these propitious moments in order to go introvert and have a peep into the inner world. There is also an imperceptibly short interval between two thoughts, and *yogīs* watchfully concentrate on this state in an attempt to pass into *nirvikalpa samādhi*, and taste the bliss of higher consciousness. This practice is known as *unmeṣa dhāraṇā*. Clear references to these practices are met with more than once in the book. The author prayed, "Be Thou manifest to me, O Lord, out of exulation or grief, out of a pillar or a pitcher, out of external objects or from within."[1] This and similar other verses give us a clue to the line of *sādhanā* adopted by the author.

Meditation is the art of tuning oneself to a higher state of being, and is not for one who does not know all that it implies. A *sādhaka* must be sufficiently awakened (*prabuddha*) to be able to set his mind on the object of meditation. In fact, the aim of meditation is to lead an awakened person to the state of a fully awakened (*suprabuddha*) one. Through this the mind is able to peep into the mysterious world of the spirit. When the glimpse enlarges, the mind begins to feel the divine presence on all sides and in all that a *sādhaka* senses. The whole world becomes the manifested symbol of the unmanifested.

The Lord takes care of all those, whose self-surrender is absolute and unreserved. He cannot forsake those who consider Him as their sole refuge. The author declared, "This the

1. Verse 5/10.

Lord, the master of the three *śaktis*, is my father, and *Bhavānī*, my mother. To me there is no second in the world."[1] His sincerity, earnestness and devotion bore fruit when he started having occasional flashes of the light of consciousness. These flashes, though steeped in immortal bliss, made him all the more restless as they were fleeting and did not endure. They have been recorded by him thus : "Thy vision, which, O Lord, comes to me off and on like a flash of lightning, steeped in immortal bliss, should it come to stay, Thou wouldst be rightly worshipped. What else should I need ?"[2] These occasional experiences filled his being with divine thrill. During the short spell of these experiences he realized his identity as the fount of supreme joy, but soon after he lost the thread of his awareness, and the relative world began to re-appear in all its diversity, and began to overwhelm him. He felt sore like a fish out of water or one robbed of all his treasures, and mourned his loss. He sang piteously like a bird that had lost its mate in the solitary woods. His plaintive notes are unsurpassed in their impressiveness and emotional content. He expressed his feelings in a language that can do credit to any literary talent in the world. He produced through words life-like pictures of his feelings, emotions and experiences. Maddened with love he invoked the Lord's grace to make those fleeting experiences an integral part of his being, and also continued his efforts till he attained his goal. We can very well observe from various verses in the book how hard put to it the author was to attain unqualified *samādhi*, and to make it a permanent possession. He ascended the highest rung of spiritual ladder by dint of strenuous effort, but was pulled down again and again by forces of nature. He exclaimed, "Having step by step scaled the various rungs of the ladder of divinities, and having even clasped the adorable feet of *Śiva,* ah, I still do not part with the lower plane."[3] He is all praise for devotees who are triumphant in the Herculean task of maintaining the thread of awareness in all states of consciousness and in all conditions of life. He extols them thus, "They

1. Verse 19/17.
2. Verse 4/8.
3. Verse 4/2.

are the overlords even of *Brahmā* and others, they are worthy of all blessedness, those who in dream as in deep sleep maintain the festival of Thy worship."[1] A daring adventurer that he was, he was not satisfied with partial experience of the great truth. He carried his quest to a bitter end, and delved deep into the world of the spirit till a *paśu* became the *Pati*, master of the two worlds.

In fact, the whole book is a narrative of the author's struggle between *samādhi* and *vyutthāna*. The mind drags him back from the state of supreme bliss into the world of disharmony, and he is at a loss to understand why. Filled with wonder he addressed the Lord thus : "Oh, is there a joy or a power on earth higher than the experience of oneness with Thee ? Wherefore, then, doth the mind of Thy devotees stray into wrong channels leaving that behind ?"[2] He loved and wooed his Lord, and with directness of expression addressed to him all his doubts, sorrows and feelings, and he got the answer in due time. He was steeped in the bliss of love, and with this as his only weapon he was able to subdue all his adversaries on the battlefield of life. He made determined efforts to realize his true self in *nirvikalpa samādhi*, and was subsequently able to recognize the world outside as his own mainfestation, and to claim, "I roar, and, lo, I dance. My dream has come true, having realized Thee, My Lord of exquisite beauty."[3] According to the commentator the verse signifies the author's entry into what is known as *vismaya mudrā*, which is a prelude to the attainment of the final goal of spiritual quest.

Liberation: what it implies

The ultimate end of all spiritual endeavour, according to all the systems of Indian philosophy, is the attainment of *mokṣa* or liberation. But the conception of liberation varies with each system. The *Sāṅkhyas* hold that bondage is the conjunction of *puruṣa* with *prakṛti* and their disjunction is what they call

1. Verse 17/7.
2. Verse 4/17.
3. Verse 3/11.

kaivalyam, the soul remaining alone. Some others call it *duḥkhānta* or cessation of pain. Evidently, these are negative concepts, but liberation is something positive. According to some others it is the emergence of a state in which the individual comes to realize his true nature as different from the body and other coverings. According to *Śaivism*, however, mere realization of the self is not the end, but a stage in spiritual evolution corresponding to the state of *vijñānākalas* characterized by the development of *jñāna śakti*. *Mokṣa* has been defined by Abhinavagupta as the unfoldment of all the potentialities of the self consequent on the cutting asunder of all the knots of ignorance. In the rope of ignorance there are numberless knots which are nothing other than non-realization of the self. The first, of these is the identification of the self with the body, the mind and the *prāṇas*. The second is the differentiation of the world from the self. Similarly, there is the differentiation of the beings among themselves and of the individual self from the Universal. These knots give rise to mistaken ideas and are responsible for the cycle of birth and death through which one is made to pass. A man is not redeemed unless knots are untied one after another, and the bliss of realization experienced in *samādhi*. Liberation is another name of realization, and is not something to be achieved anew. The self is ever free and bondage is a mere delusion. The greatest bondage is the certainty that there is bondage. This is just an attitude of mind and unless this is overcome with the light of knowledge there can be no liberation. Self-realization, though an important achievement and a necessary step in spiritual progress, is not the end. It is mistaken by some as the last step in spiritual progress. Perfect *siddhi* is the attainment of a state conforming to that of *Śiva* Himself. This implies mastery over the powers of *icchā*, *jñāna* and *kriyā*, and, as such, is the highest stage in spiritual evolution. In order to attain this state one has to pass through various levels of consciousness corresponding to those of *Brahmā*, *Viṣṇu* *Īśvara* and *Sadāśiva*. Very early in his life the author had set his mind on this stage as the goal of his strivings, and, as such, earnestly longed to have ever new experiences till his dream was fully realized. He was not satisfied with the mere realization of his identity as distinct from the body and other sheaths. His lure to explore the higher levels of consciousness made him plunge his whole being into the effort and grapple with the forces of lower nature that thwarted his further progress. This is like sailing on a tempestuous sea against strong currents, and calls for great daring and perseverence. The heroic struggle undertaken by the author to attain this end and the obstacles encountered on the way have been recorded by him in unequivocal language. Intense devotion and relentless effort are needed to overcome lower nature and to get rooted in this blessed state of consciousness. A devotee established in *Śiva* consciousness is no other than *Śiva* Himself, and is adorable as such. In fact, the book starts with an invocation not to *Śiva* but to a devotee who has attained oneness with *Śiva* without any conventional means. The author pays tribute to such devotees as superior to the Lord of creation himself. He asks, "From amongst *Brahmā* and others, even from amongst *Brahmarṣis*, who is equal to the happy soul ever enjoying the nectar of Thy worship ?"[1]

Ignorance, which is the root cause of bondage, can only be dispelled by the light of knowledge. In the absence of knowledge even *samādhī* is fruitless. Knowledge is of two kinds, theoretical and practical. The former is gained by the study of scriptures or listening to the teaching of a *guru*, while practical knowledge is the direct result of *samādhi*. Both of these are indispensable for recognition. A man having neither theoretical knowledge of jewels nor practical experience will not be able to recognize one. Similarly, a man possessing no theoretical knowledge or practical experience will not be able to recognize his own nature by momentary *samādhis* encountered in daily life. Even *nirvikalpa samādhi* is fruitless in the absence of theoretical knowledge. Indeterminate knowledge is simple light which is in harmony with everything and contradicts nothing. It is like a convass on which anything can be painted. After arising from this *samādhi* its memory persists, and contemplation on this enables a *yogī* to recognize himself as 'I am that'. Ignorance can only be dispelled by *savikalpa samādhi*, and this is what is known as *pratyabhijñā*.

1. Verse 17/9.

Doctrine of Recognition

Utpaladeva showed the world a new path as he claims at the end of his *Pratyabhijñā Kārikā*. This is based on the *Śiva Dṛṣṭi* of his *guru*, Somānanda. The aim of this is to explain the nature of the Ultimate Reality and the means to the attainment of the highest end of life, that is to say, freedom from the bondage of *Māyā*, the principle of obscuration. The individual self has subjected himself to limitation through ignorance of his true nature, and it is the light of consciousness that has the power to dispel it. The means to realization is not knowledge but recognition. Realization does not consist in knowing what is not known already, nor attaining something new, but penetrating through the veil of ignorance, and recognizing the individual self as *Maheśvara*. The individual is essentially free, but his freedom is clouded by ignorance, which needs to be removed in order to enable a seeker to recognize his identity with the Ultimate Reality.

Recognition is an act by which we re-call a former perception and identify it with the object actually present, a unification of a former experience with what appears now. It demands a mental picture of the object already seen or heard of, and consists in identifying it with the object present. Thus, it requires not only the previous knowledge of the object, but also its actual presence at the time being. Recognition is of various kinds, but here we are concerned with it only so far as it relates to the self. When we begin to study higher spiritual truths as contained in sacred books, there arises in our minds a picture of the Lord as possessing of supreme power as well as our identity with Him. This intellectual apprehension is a necessary pre-condition for recognition. Recognition becomes possible when the self reveals some unmistakable signs conforming to the picture already in our mind. *Pratyabhijñā* is that faculty which enables a seeker to attain self-recognition without any external help. The real nature of recognition as against knowledge is explained by the author through the illustration of a young girl who falls in love with a hero whom she has not seen but has heard of his qualities. Day and night she pants for the young hero, and is consumed by pangs of separation. She sends letters and messengers to the young hero to come and satisfy her desire. Incidentally, the hero appears before her one day, but she cannot recognize him, and as such fails to derive any satisfaction from the presence of her beloved who appears to her as a common man. Similarly, though the Lord is shining within as the self of all, His mere presence cannot give satisfaction unless His powers of unchecked knowledge and action are fully recognized. When a man clearly recognizes the distinctive powers of the Lord, he becomes liberated in his very tife time.

Unlike *Vedānta*, *Śaivism* holds the world to be real as it is a manifestaion of the Real. It is not an illusion, and does not disappear on self-realization as the illusory serpent does when the rope is recognized as a fact. Realization does not imply negation of the facts of experience, but brings with it a new understanding and a new appreciation of the objective world. The world continues to appear even after realization, but is known in its true perspective. This is pratyabhijñā or recognition.

Realization and After

The experience of higher consciousness starts from the waking state and is apt to be lost in the other two states of dream and deep sleep. Waking is the most important state of consciousness being the field of *sādhanā* and the starting point of *siddhi*. A *sādhaka* who has attained *siddhi* in the wakeful state and acquired the powers attendant on it is known as *prabuddha* (awakened). After having consolidated his gains on this plane, the next step is to extend his sway on the worlds of dream and deep sleep, and to attain what is known as *svapna svātantryam* by remaining in unbroken awareness of the self in all states of consciousness. He is then known as *suprabuddha* (fully awakened).

After having his first glimpses of the inner self, the author made supreme effort to maintain the thread of awareness uninterrupted in the wakeful state, and then addressed himself to the difficult task of extending his domain over the other two states. But soon he lost his identity and the strong current of past impressions carried him helplessly on to the distant shores of a strange world of dreams. When he regained his wakeful state, he felt despondent, and addressed himself to the Lord thus : "One with Thee I am, firmly established in Thy worship.

Though ceaselessly worshipping thus, wherefore do I not involuntarily maintain the same poise even in the state of dreams ?"[1] The world of dreams is by far the more difficult to conquer than the physical world. Superhuman effort is needed to overcome the impressions of past thoughts and ideas, and to induct the light and bliss of *turīyā* into the three lower planes. When a *sādhaka* is firmly established in self-realization, and has acquired a poise of freedom from the mind he can move from one plane to another without losing his experience of absolute bliss. Says the author, "Waking, dream or deep sleep—whatever the state—to the lover with mind fully merged in Thee all this is a great festival."[2]

An extraordinary devotee that he was, the author was not disheartened by temporary set-backs, but was determined to carry his struggle to a finish till he was able to maintain firm hold over the various planes within his personality.

When the experience of higher consciousness becomes constant as a result of relentless effort, it is called *nityodita* or *sahaja samādhi* from which there is no return into the plane of relative existence. *Samādhi* may be introverted (*nimīlana*) or extroverted (*unmīlana*). In the former a *yogī* is not aware of anything other than the self, while in the other the consciousness of the body and the world outside persists without affecting the *yogī's* spiritual poise. The *yogī* does not associate himself with the body, and the relative universe does not shake his unitive experience. He looks upon the world as his own play, his own divine *līlā*. It is said in the *Spanda Kārikā*, "He who possesses this sort of consciousness, or he who regards this universe as a play and is always united, is beyond doubt liberated in life."[3] When the two forms of *samādhi* are realized as identical, the realization is complete and one becomes master of the two worlds.

In the first lap of *sādhanā* the world of matter including the body and the mind has to be viewed as separate till one attains a poise of freedom from them, and realizes one's identity in unqualified *samādhi*. Such persons need not draw their mind

1. Verse 11/5
2. Verse 18/16
3. Spanda Kārikā 2/5

and senses away from the world as everything is integrated into the being of the Lord. They behold the whole world as their own manifestation, all the while remaining in unmitigated awareness of their identity. They are no longer deluded by subject-object relations, and maintain simultaneous sway over the two worlds. They continue to lead the life of the world while rooted in the bliss of consciousness. Having mastered the *Śaktis* of *jñāna* and *kriyā,* they are capable of staying in any plane of existence without losing their awareness. This form of *samādhi* is undoubtedly the last word in spiritual perfection, and is extremely difficult of attainment. *Mahātmās* living in this blessed state, though not a few, hardly come into limelight, and walk the earth almost *incognito* just to grace mankind out of their abundant compassion. The author extols them every now and then as worthy of highest respect, and says, "Lord, hundreds indeed are the rare souls, who, at Thy own inspiration, while following pursuits of ploughmen do behold Thy form face to face with these very eyes."[1] Being the meeting point of the two worlds this state is technically known as *madhya bhūmi,* and falls to the lot of some rare *mahātmās,* whose chain of transmigration has already come to an end, but still have a mission in the world.

The author disparages the form of *samādhi* in which a *yogī* concentrates on the inner self to the exclusion of all else and is virtually lost to the world. To such a *yogī* the world of relative experience presents a formidable barrier, while a devotee remains poised even in *vyutthāna.* The author draws a contrast between the two types of *yogīs,* and says, "Left alone, who cannot cognize Thee, Lord, while the objective world has dissolved itself (in *samādhi*) ? To the devotee, on the other hand, Thou art clearly visible even during the confusion of the subject and the object."[2] A devotee enjoys the whole creation as the Lord's play in a spirit of participation, associating himself with all that it implies. In his *Īśvara Pratyabhijñā Kārikā* the author declares, "He who has realized his identity with the universe and knows

1. Verse 12/21.
2. Verse 1/8.

that all that is manifest is his glory, is the highest Lord even when determinate cognitions are still rising."[1]

After attaining *siddhi* the author did not prefer to be lost in unqualified *samādhi*. The milk of human kindness was flowing in his veins and as such he preferred to remain on the threshold of the two worlds, enjoying divine presence and at the same time helping deserving seekers in the realization of the *Maheśvara* of the self. His *Īśvara Pratyabhijñā* was written during this supra-mental state. The author did not belong to the category of saints who are concerned with their own salvation and for whom the world at large has no use. The idea of liberation as a personal gain did not fit in with his aim in life. Even the over-lordship of the two worlds held no charm for him. He viewed things in a different perspective, and the little self did not enter into consideration. He did not seek liberation away from the world, but preferred to live in the company of his fellow beings, and to enjoy the fruit of his strivings with all. Even in the stage of *sādhanā* he had the good of mankind at heart, or, one might say, he undertook *sādhanā* not merely for his little self, but for the benefit of the world as a whole. This is clearly borne out by this verse, "When shall I, O Lord, in the height of exultation, reveal to all the treasure of Thy holy feet, abruptly obtained and firmly grasped"?[2] The author did not make secret either of his aspirations or his achievements. Spiritual attainment does not imply a state in which man has no obligations towards humanity as a whole. In fact, a spiritually advanced man has greater responsibility for the welfare of his fellow beings. He is great in proportion to the service he renders to others. A devotee over-flows with compassion for his fellow beings, and utilizes his spiritual gains not only for himself, but also for the good of all humanity. Says the author, "With the mind abloom as a result of Thy full blooded vision the selfless movements and sayings of *mahātmās* come into play as a mere sport."[3] Spiritual life is not inconsistent with activity. The activities of the liberated are free and spontaneous.

---

1. *Īśvara Pratyabhijñā Kārikā*, Tattva-Saṅgraha Adhikāra, verse 12.
2. Verse 9/10.
3. Verse 12/7.

There is no smooth passage to spiritual fulfilment. The path is beset with difficulties and needs earnestness and perseverence. It is like walking on the sharp edge of a razor and demands greatest vigilance so as to obviate the risk of a fall. Mere control of thought process does not constitute the end. A complete stillness of mind is generally followed by total disappearance of the objective world with no positive gain. This kind of negative experience is described in some books as *śūnya bhūmi* and is commonly met with by *yogīs* during the course of *sādhanā*. There is a sort of trackless wilderness between the two worlds of senses and that of consciousness in which many a *sādhaka* has floundered. One must go beyond this in order to have a positive experience of the Ultimate Truth, which is not a void but a reality. This entails Herculean effort and calls for divine grace. The author seems to have this state in mind when he exclaimed, "This horrifying world has, as it were, come to an end; the heavy dross of the mind has melted away; still, there is, O Lord, not the least opening in the bolted panels of Thy city gates." The mind became blank and there was complete darkness with no trace of light. The objective world passed into oblivion, yet there was no positive experience of the Supreme Self. There is nothing peculiar in an experience of this kind, but one must go beyond this in order to know the whole truth. Sri Aurobindo had this experience when he successfully controlled the *vṛttis* of the mind under the guidance of his *guru*, the Marhatta *yogī*, Lele. Positive experience came to him spontaneously after several months when he was confined within the four walls of Alipore Jail. He felt the presence of the Lord in everything around himself. Paramahaṁsa Rāmakṛṣṇa was saved by *Mother Kālī* Herself. It is said that during his *yogic sādhanā* his *suṣumṇā nāḍī* opened all of a sudden and a quantity of blood began to rush upwards. But instead of rushing towards the brain the blood made a passage through the palate, and rushed out into the mouth where it got clogged. The happening caused sensation in the Dakṣiṇeśvara temple where he was staying. A *yogī*, who happened to be there at the time examined the colour of the blood and congratulated the Paramahaṁsa saying that it was fortunate for him that the blood did not rush into the brain. Otherwise, he would have passed into *jaḍa samādhi*, from which it would have been impossible for him to return into physical consciousness.

The author continued his struggle relentlessly. He was determined to carry his struggle to a bitter end mindless of any obstacles that might come in his way. He found the Lord's citadel closed on all sides and did not know how to get in. Aloud he cried and appealed to the Lord in tones which are at once pathetic, thought-provoking and full of devotional fervour. His agony broke out in words of magic that touch the deepest chords of the human heart. He cried, "Lord, wherefore dost Thou not lend ear to my wailings?"[1] Drunk with the wine of divine love he continued his efforts with redoubled vigour, but still there was no opening of the portals. He squatted in front of the gateway, and prayed, "Where Thou along with Thy consort stayeth from the mansion house to the city gates—of that sanctuary of Thine, oh, would I be a denizen."[2] Again, "With the heart pining to behold the core of the ever blooming lotus of Thy countenance, deign, O Lord, to appear face to face before me."[3] He looked forward to the moment when he could "with a bang breaking asunder all strong door pins"[4] step into the Lord's presence. He appealed to the Lord to seize him by the collar and hurl him into the sanctuary of his being. In course of time he found himself out of the wilderness and tried to delve deep into his being as identical with the Lord. But the Lord played hide and seek with him. He caught occasional glimpses, and when they receded, he became sad, and complained, "Even after having come within my ken wherefore dost Thou, O Lord, elude me, Thy servant? To what creature dost Thou not form a moment's object of sight?"[5]

We can see clearly how the author progressed from one stage to another, what obstacles came in his way and how heroically he managed to overcome them till he reached the acme of spiritual excellence. How the gate opened on him, and how he sang and danced in the Lord's presence with "Hari, Brahmā

1. Verse 4/19.
2. Verse 5/7.
3. Verse 4/16.
4. Verse 9/3.
5. Verse 12/16.

and Indra helplessly waiting outside" is the burden of these songs. A glimpse enlarged into a vision; a spark became a flame. He stood face to face with God, addressing Him in unsophisticated language. In His audience chamber he sings like a golden oriole, and his feelings of exultation and sorrow find expression in songs of divine melody. To him *Śiva* is not a silent spectator, in whose presence the inexplicable *Māyā* plays the game of the world. His Lord is possessed of sovereign will and is not indifferent to the wailing of His devotees. He is not bound by any laws conceivable by man. Creation and dissolution are His mere sports, divine *līlā*. He is the Supreme Controller, without whose pleasure not a thought can arise in the human heart. Such a Lord cannot but be possessed of exquisite beauty and be an object of love. He is *Hara*, the captivator of hearts, in whose presence all desires melt away, and yearning for liberation becomes meaningless.

Śaktipāta

All through the course of *sādhanā* the author felt the presence of an invisible hand that inspired and led him progressively on to the goal of God realization, and awakened in him a painful yet inexpressibly delightful yearning to have ever new experiences of the various stages of this arduous journey.

The Ultimate Reality is self-luminous, and does not stand in need of any external light to illumine it. It is an experiencing principle that cannot form an object of our knowledge. Self-realization as such is not a case of man realizing God, but one of God revealing Himself through the instrumentality of His divine power or *Śakti*. All actions, physical or mental, reflect His will. No one can advance on the path of *Śiva* except with some sort of an impulse from this *Śakti*. Sometimes, this impulse is so sudden that one is startled and sometimes so gradual that one is hardly aware of it. This is known as the doctrine of *Śaktipāta* or descent of *Śakti*. Śrī Śaṅkarācārya fully endorses this view. In his famous work, *Viveka-Cūḍāmaṇi* he says, "These three, so difficult of attainment, are acquired by the grace of the Lord : birth as man, desire for liberation and contact with great souls."[1]

1. *Viveka-Cūḍāmaṇi*, verse 3.

The Lord is absolutely free and his sovereign will is not bound by any consideration. No conditions are attached to His grace. In the words of Baba Farid, "His grace may fall on us at any time. There are no definite rules regulating it. Some do not get it after performing great austerities and night-long vigils while it is forced on those who lie asleep."[1]

Love is never unilateral. It emanates simultaneously in the lover and the loved. Says the author, "Thou art pleased with devotion, and devotion emanates at Thy pleasure. How the two are related Thou alone knoweth,"[2] True love is always inspired by God. In the words of Gālib, "It is a fire that can neither be kindled nor extinguished." When love-itch gets intensified, man becomes restless till he rubs his shoulder with the Lord. How it sets in and how it attains consummation are things that have remained unanswered through the ages.

Mukti is the state of *Śiva* and *sādhanā* the sphere of *Śakti*. *Śiva* is recognized through His *Śaktis* in the same way as the sun is known through its light. *Śakti* is said to be the gateway to *Śiva*. In fact, all spiritual effort is the domain of *Śakti*, which must be invoked till one attains a state of absolute freedom, when *Śiva* and *Śakti* are realized as one, two facets of the same reality. Says the author, "Thou dominateth one state, another is dominated by Thy consort, containing within Her bosom the whole order of material creation. In the final analysis, there is no difference betwixt Thy consort, Thyself and the triune world."[3] What is commonly known as realization is only the development of *Jñāna Śakti*. The next step is that of *Kriyā Śakti*, which implies entrance into what is known as the pure path *Śuddhādhvā* characterized by the attainment of all *siddhis*. The two *Śaktis* of *jñāna* and *kriyā* are of great importance in the path of spirituality, as they enable a *sādhaka* to overcome limitations of *Māyā*, and to know or to do anything at his will. They are symbolically represented by the two feet of the Lord that the author so often invokes in the book. After attaining self-

1. Bankey Behary: *Sufis, Mystics and Yogis of India*, p. 105 (Bharatiya Vidya Bhavan, Bombay)
2. Verse 16/21.
3. Verse 18/2.

realization a true seeker cannot afford to be complacent, and must continue his efforts till he enters the pure path and assumes an altogether new identity. Any laxity in the effort can bring about what may be called a spiritual debacle. The author seems to have had a difficult time striving to extend his domain over the Lord's *Kriyā Śaḳti*. This is clearly testified by a number of verses in which he expresses anguish over the absence of *siddhis*. Love of God, he says, is a *siddhi* par excellence, but is not perfect unless the potentialities of the self manifest themselves. These *siddhis* are concomitants of advancement in the spiritual path and are essential landmarks inasmuch as they help a *sādhaka* to know where he stands. Their failure was naturally a matter of grave concern to the author. Says he, "Love for Thee, the Lord, master of the three worlds, is verily a sublime *siddhi*, but in absence of *aṇimā* and others it is not perfect. This is my anguish."[1] Many students, who do not understand the true nature of spiritual attainments wonder that a man of the calibre of Utpaladeva should have cravings for super-natural powers. They overlook the fact that these powers inevitably appear in the advanced stages of spiritual progress indicating mastery over the Lord's *Kriyā Śakti*. All *siddhas* in the world have been possessing *siddhis* including those who have cautioned aspirants against them. *Siddhis* by themselves had no fascination for the author, but their role could not be overlooked. They are guiding stars in the unchartered ocean of consciousness, and wise *sādhakas* make judicious use of them. As time rolled by, all *siddhis* attended on the author. How he viewed them is clearly reflected by this verse, "Hold me not lightly, O Lord, as one carried away by the achievement of paltry *siddhis*; in the face of Thy love liberation itself following radiant *siddhis* is of little consequence."[2] We thus see that the author did acquire all *siddhis*, but did not attach to them more importance than they deserved.

The Ultimate Reality

The state of *Śiva* is the highest state of realization. It is a purely subjective state characterized by perfect I-consciousness

1. Verse 15/15.
2. Verse 19/14.

without a shadow of this-ness. *Śiva* is the Ultimate Reality underlying the world of name and form, and is the innermost self in all things and beings. *Śiva* is the self-luminous universal consciousness that holds within it all that constitutes the world in all its variety of forms. He illumines everything including all the known sources of light, and is not revealed by anything external to Himself. He is inscrutable, beyond the reach of mind and intellect, and is, therefore, defined by the author as the absence of all definability. He is eternal and infinite. He is all-pervading and all-transcending having a twofold aspect—an immanent one in which He pervades the whole universe and a transcendental one beyond all manifestation. Difficult of attainment even by *munis*, He is clearly realized by devotees in all quarters and all states. He is the fountainhead of all beauty, the highest and the natural object of love, the inexhaustible ocean of power, even the strollers on whose shores attain all sorts of prosperity. He is the origin and the end of the universe—a mere hoax in essence. He is sportful and through the instrumentality of His *Śakti* enacts the wonderful scene of creation on His own being without losing His transcendental character. In the order of descent (*avarohakrama*) He conceals His own form, subjects Himself to limitation, and appears in countless forms, the sentient and the insentient, the gross and the subtle, while in the order of ascent (*ārohakrama*) He reveals Himself as the change less reality beyond bondage and liberation. He remains untainted like a lotus growing on the thick mire of material creation. He is the author of the *vedas* and *āgamas*, yet opposed to them.

Śiva is the highest metaphysical principle described as light and intelligence (*Prakāśavimarśamaya*). The two aspects are inseparable from each other, and apply equally to the individual self which is the same in essence as the Universal self. *Prakāśa* is that aspect of the self which is responsible for a vague reflection of external objects as at the time of instant perception through the senses or revival of past impressions as at the time of imagination or dream. This is compared to a mirror which is capable of receiving external light to illumine it while the self shines independent of any external light. This is indeterminate cognition (*nirvikalpa jñāna*). *Vimarśa* is the distinctive aspect of the self. It is the power of deliberation which cognizes objects in all their aspects and gives rise to determinate cognition (*savikalpa jñāna*). The latter again is of two kinds. One is the immediate cognition, and the other, the impression left on the mind known as memory. Dreamless sleep is characterized by *prakāśa* only without *vimarśa*, while the wakeful state is characterized by both. *Nirvikalpa samādhi*, *suṣupti* and instant cognition are alike, being characterized by pre-dominance of *prakāśa* and absence of *vimarśa*. *Vimarśa* is the power of the self to know itself in all its purity, to create new impressions, to recall and control the existing stock of *saṁskāras*. The Universal self differs from the individual self only so far as the latter receives its reflections not only from external causes, but also from the internal, while the former being all-inclusive cannot be affected by any external cause. It is this *vimarśa* which is spoken of as the *Svātantrya Śakti* of the Lord, and is responsible for manifestation of the universe as apparently separate while holding everything in perfect identity with itself. The Lord's freedom lies in the fact that He does not depend on anything external to Himself for bringing the universe into manifestation. The universe is His mere *ābhāsa* (idea), and is like a picture drawn on the smooth screen of Universal Consciousness. It is related to the Lord as a dream world is related to the individual self. The Lord projects the universe on the background of His *prakāśa* aspect, manifests the thirty-six categories constituting the body and the universe of matter in all its diversity, brings about endless creations by uniting and separating the *ābhāsas* of time and space. Each one of the categories is an *ābhāsa* except the first which is the substratum of the rest, and the entire creation owes its birth to the peculiar combination of these. The universe is what exists in the divine mind. Creation merely consists in manifesting as apparently separate what is already in the Universal self, and dissolution is nothing but its merging back into the subjective state. It is only the objective state that is seemingly created and destroyed, while the subjective state remains unchanged. *Śiva* awakens, the universe, potentially existing within Him, becomes patent. He goes to sleep, the same is drawn back and rests within Him in potential form. He is thus the material as well as the efficient cause of creation. *Prakāśa* is the former and *vimarśa*, the latter. The two are inseparably connected.

Śakti, the dynamic aspect of the Lord

The Lord is *Maheśvara* and the universe, His *Śakti.* They are two aspects of the same Reality and are inseparably connected. *Śakti* is related to *Śiva* as light is to the sun. Through Her instrumentality the Lord performs the five acts (*pañcakṛtyas*) of manifestation, maintenance, withdrawal, obscuration and grace. Though one, She assumes innumerable forms, the chief among them being *Cit*, *Ānanda*, *Icchā*, *Jñāna* and *Kriyā* corresponding to the five states of *Śiva*, *Śakti*, *Sadāśiva*, *Īśvara* and *Śuddha Vidyā*. She is the grand matrix that like the seed of a banyan tree or the egg of a peahen holds within her the potentialities of creation in all its vastness and multiplicity. She is the material as well as the efficient cause of the world, which is merely the Lord's sport. She is infinite and the inexhaustible storehouse of energy, beyond time and space. In the boundless ocean of *Śakti* or *Mahāmāyā* countless universes float like so many bubbles. Creation and dissolution play on Her lap. She is responsible for both liberation and bondage, the order of descent and the order of ascent. In the former She assumes the form of matter and *Śiva* becomes a *paśu* while in the latter the *paśu* loses its trammels and re-discovers himself as *Śiva* Himself. *Śakti* is the entrance into the kingdom of God, and a devotee must invoke Her help for the success of his endeavours. Without Her grace perfect *siddhi* will remain a hollow dream. When a *Sādhaka* contacts *Śakti* he acquires the powers of Śiva, which transform his whole being, and the *paśu* becomes *Pati*, Maheśvara Himself.

The manifestation of *Śiva* is broadly divided into *Śuddhādhvā* (pure path) and *aśuddhādhvā* (impure path). There are four states of universal experience known as *Śiva*, *Sadāśiva*, *Īśvara* and *Śuddha Vidyā*, and the experients are *Śiva*, *Mantra Maheśvara*, *Mantreśvara* or *Vidyeśvaras* or *Mantras* respectively. The states of limited individual experience are *Vijñānakalās*, *Pralayakalās* and *sakalās* respectively. These constitute the seven *pramatṛs* or experients from *Śiva* down to *sakalā*, and represent different levels of consciousness. When the Lord gives up His state of oneness, and desires to manifest the creation on His own being by mystifying His own nature, His power of intelligence (*vimarśa*) is reduced to volition (*icchā*) and later into knowledge (*jñāna*) and action (*kriyā*). The power of knowledge is the determination as 'this is that and not otherwise'. The power of action comes next, and is represented by the expression, 'let this whole be thus'. These powers are responsible for the whole phenomena of creation. In this process the category of *Sadāśiva* comes first. At this stage the internal aspect (*āntara daśā*) or the power of knowledge dominates, and the consciousness of being rises for the first time. It is the concretization of *cit* and consists in the this-consciousness of the mass of objects on the part of subjects technically known as *Mantra Maheśvaras*. The consciousness of this-ness, however, is not clear, but is vague on account of the pre-dominance of I-Consciousness, and this is, therefore, represented as I-this. When the external aspect (*bahirbhāva*) or the power of action comes to prominence, the universe attains clarity to the sentient beings called *Mantreśvaras*. This is the state of *Īśvara*. In the former stage this-consciousness is obscure, while in the latter it is clear. This state is represented by the expression this-I. The fourth stage is that of *Śuddha Vidyā* (pure knowledge) in which the mass of objects, though pure consciousness, yet appears as distinct from the self. The subjects in this state are called *Vidyeśvaras* or *Mantras* who are governed by *Ananta Bhaṭṭāraka*. The *Vidyeśvaras* are fully aware of their identity, but the objects are mistaken to be different. In fact, *Śuddha Vidyā* is the resting of both I-consciousness and this-consciousness on a common substratum. In the state of *paśu* it is this *vidyāśakti* that reveals the true nature of the Lord, and as such holds an important stage in spiritual evolution.

Now comes the stage of *Māyā*, known as impure path. *Māyā Śakti* is that power of the Lord which is responsible for misapprehension in regard to the subject and the object. It is capable of accomplishing what is most difficult. It is the power of delusion that makes the subjects identify themselves with *Śūnya*, *buddhi*, *prāṇa* and the physical body forgetting the real self, and causes undiluted differentiation. The limited subjects know the limited objects only. They are conditioned by five sheaths (*kañcukas*) of *kāla*, *vidyā*, *kalā*, *rāga* and *niyati*. *Kāla* is responsible for the sense of succession, *vidyā* for limited knowledge, *Kalā* for limited doership, *rāga* for the choice of one thing to the exclusion of another, and *niyati* for fixed results from fixed causes. The subject limited by five *kañcukas* in addition to that of *Māyā* is said to be the *puruṣa*. At this stage consciousness loses its omnipotence and omniscience and is limited by three *malas* (impurities) which are the creation of *Māyā Śakti* of the Lord. The subject is, therefore called *paśu*, one bound by the chains of *Māyā*.

The *puruṣa*, that is, the limited subject must have a limited field for its limited powers of knowledge and action. This consists of means and objects, twenty three in number. They are the products of *prakṛti* or *pradhāna*, which is their root cause. *Prakṛti* is the state of identity of the three *guṇas* of *sattva*, *rajas* and *tamas*, which are the causes of pleasure, pain and delusion respectively. The intellect, the mind and the ego are the internal senses (*antaḥkaraṇa*). The intellect is the faculty of determination, the mind constitutes thought, emotion and desires. The five senses limit the power of knowledge, and the five organs restrict the power of action of the subject. The five *tanmātras* of sound, touch, sight, taste and smell are all the effects of *prakṛti*. These combine to form what are called the five gross elements (*mahābhūtas*) which go into the making of gross bodies and the physical world.

These, in short, are the thirty-six categories accepted by the system as forming the order of creation These are *ābhāsas* except the first which is the basis of all other *ābhāsas*. When the Lord gives up His state of oneness and manifests the diversity of forms He subjects His power of *icchā*, *jñāna* and *kriyā* to limitations. These limitations are called *malas* (impurities). He first limits His power of will and this is called *āṇava mala*. It consists in the obscuration of the powers of omnipotence and omniscience. This is of two kinds, that is to say, omniscience, without omnipotence and omnipotence without omniscience. This limits the self, which is, therefore, called *aṇu*. There are subjects, who are pure consciousness and full of omniscience without the power of freedom. They are called *vijñānākalas* or *vijñānakevalins*. They are above the sphere of *Māyā* and below *śuddhavidyā*. They have got only one *mala* and are free from transmigratory existence. The limitation brought about in the power of knowledge is the *Māyīya mala*, which is responsible for consciousness of objects as distinct from the self. The limitation in the power of action is known as *kārma mala*. It arises in the form of merit and demerit as a result of the consciousness of the external world as separate from oneself. This *mala* is mainly responsible for transmigration. The other two limited subjects are *pralayākalas* and *sakalas*. The former are those, whose I-consciousness shines in relation to *śūnya*, *prāṇa* or *buddhi*. They have the two impurities of *āṇava* and *kārma* while that of *Māyā* may or may not be there. They are without bodies and senses and are almost insentient. They remain in that condition as long as the universe lasts, and get connected with bodies and senses after the dissolution. Then there are subjects possessing all the three *malas*. They are transmigratory beings known as *sakalas*. Thus, we have seven *pramātṛs* from *Śiva* to *sakala*. The first four are pure subjects, and the last three, limited.

Theory of Knowledge

The Supreme Lord as the embodiment of consciousness holds within Him all that can be perceived or conceived of exactly as an individual holds the dream world within himself. The objective state has no existence apart from the cognizing subject, and represents the same light of consciousness that holds together the objects and the cognizing subject. The relation between the subject and the object is not that between two independent entities, as, in that case, they will remain totally cut off from each other, and the subject will remain unaware of the objective world. According to the author all that exists is light : nothing can exist outside this. Light is the very nature of things. The subject and the objects are one in essence, manifestations of the same light as waves are that of water. Cognition is nothing but meeting of the subjective and objective waves in the sea of universal consciousness. The very act of cognition implies some sort of kinship between the subject and the objects perceived. In the absence of this there can be no cognition. Knowledge presupposes unity between the knower and the known. There can be no relation between two mutually exclusive entities such as light and darkness. Says Dr. Radhakrisnan, "The dualism of the mind and the external world, whatever truth it may have at the psychological level, is overcome when we rise to the standpoint of logic astheory of knowledge. If the two, subject and object, the individual mind and the independent reality, are separate, then there can be no knowledge at all. Either knowledge is arbitrary and groundless or the dualism is wrong. Subject and object are not separate existences held together by an external bond. They are unity in diversity, duality in unity. The distinction of subject and object is not a relation between two independent entities, but a distinction made by knowledge within its own fold."[1]

To the author all things appeared as bound together by the same light of consciousness. He realized oneness of existence not on the intellectual level, but experienced it directly through his whole being. Says he, "But for Thy luminous form, nothing is capable of being perceived. Thus, though veiled by nature, Thou, O Lord, art ever within sight."[2]

The Upāyas

There are three *upāyas* or means mentioned in *āgamic* texts as leading to *samāveśa* as it is generally called. These are : *āṇava*, *śākta* and *śāmbhava* correspomding to the *kriyā, jñāna* and *icchā śaktis* of the Lord respectively. *Āṇava* is that form of *sādhanā* which involves utterance of *mantras*, mental disciplines, meditation on various centers of the body including control of *prāṇa*. This *upāya* is suitable for those whose mind and intellect are not sufficiently evolved to apprehend the Supreme Truth. In *Śiva Sūtras* it occupies the last chapter, while in the *Spanda* and *Pratyabhijñā Kārikās* it finds no mention whatsoever. The author calls this as material means (*Māyīyopaya*). Since *Māyā* is the principle of darkness it cannot directly lead one to enlightenment. Nonetheless, it has its own importance as a step towards the path of progress. It is characterized by the power of action and as such is also termed as *kriyopāya*. *Śāktopāya* is psychological approach to the truth of existence and is meant for devotees of sharp intellect and a highly sensitive mind. This is characterized by the power of knowledge and is also known as *jñānopāya*. This *upāya* suits such seekers as are endowed with inquisitive mind, whose power of reasoning is sufficiently deve-

1. Radhakrishnan: *Indian Philosophy*, vol.1, p. 306.
2. Verse 4/6.

loped and who are eager to discover the Supreme Truth for themselves. An aspirant is struck by apparent contradictions in the world, disharmony, darkness and suffering, and strives to probe into their causes in an attempt to overcome them and to pass from limited existence into the domain of freedom and eternal bliss independent of external objects. He studies the revealed texts, philosophical literature and the sayings of sages who have known the Reality for themselves. He approaches wise men for initiation into the mystic truths, and discusses with them the secret doctrines in order to gain true insight into their import. This gives him strength to delve deeper into the mysteries of consciousness, and have intuitional apprehension of the Reality. Constant practice, profound meditation and intense devotion are needed to realize the truth and translate it into practical experience. This is a mission of exploring the upper reaches of consciousness, and it was this heroic undertaking that the author followed and for which he was well qualified by nature.

Intellectual understanding (*Bauddha jñāna*), though not an end in itself, plays a valuable role in *sādhanā* and self-recognition. It is a preparation for direct realization as it infuses strength into the effort. Says the author, "Let deep insight into Thy profound thought dawn on me in the first instance. Having gained strength thereby, let me become endlessly engaged in Thy worship,"[1] Intellectual knowledge is essential for self-recognition.

The author referred to his cult of *bhakti* variously as the path of *Śiva*, *Maheśvara* or *Śaṅkara*, the highest metaphysical principle. Technically, it is *Śāktopāya*, the path of *Parā Śakti*, the fountain-head of all knowledge, spiritual or otherwise. *Śiva* becomes known through his *Śaktis* in the same way as the sun is known by its rays. Knowledge is inseparably connected with speech, and as such it is called *Parā Vāk* (trascendental speech) which germinally holds within it all *vedas*, *āgamas*, mundane arts and sciences in all their varieties. In fact, it is the repository of all that we call knowledge. The same speech materializes into *paśyantī*, where the words and their meanings are not distinguished, the objects being one with the subject as in the state of *Sadāśiva*.

Verse 12/23.

In the intervening stage or *madhyamā* the words and their meanings are differentiated from each other in the mind before being uttered by various places in the vocal organ. This is the stage of *vaikharī*, the source of all knowledge in the world. A devotee contemplates on the self by means of a definite concept or a *mantra* as it is called, and passes step by step from *vaikharī* into the stage of *Parā Śakti*, or *Parā Vāk* or simply Parā when he finds himself as well as the whole world as identical with *Śiva*. This is known as the stage of *Śakti* (*Śakti avasthā*) which is known as the gateway to Śiva (*Śaivimukham*).

The author acquired the powers of the Lord one after another. First of all he mastered the *Śakti* of *jñāna*, and then invoked the Lord's *kriyā śakti* as "the light of all lights, full of self-consciousness 'all this I am' that *kriyā Śakti* of Thine, O Lord, I praise."[1] He was out to extend his sway over all the powers inhering in the self so as to attain the highest point in spiritual evolution.

In the path of knowledge realization comes gradually in the course of striving. It calls for profound meditation which in turn leads to cognition and touch of Divinity. This is *Śākta samāveśa*, and involves strenuous effort to induce and maintain it. When a devotee gets rooted in this realization his whole vision is changed, and the whole universe appears as full of beauty and eternal joy.

A man of the world, whose powers of knowledge and action are circumscribed, is not capable of making any progress in the spiritual field unless inspiration is derived from within. As a result of this contact with the Divinity of the self, his powers are aroused and he is able to know or to do anything according to his will. He ceases to associate himself with his body, mind, *buddhi* or *prāṇa* and recognizes himself as the reality underlying the whole phenomena of creation. His vision undergoes total change.

There are some privileged souls to whom the experience of higher consciousness comes like a flood washing away the impurities of the mind. Flood gates of ecstasy are thrown open, and realization flows in like a torrent. The seeker finds himself drowned in an ocean of bliss, and is rather stunned to discover the

1. Verse 20/16.

whole world as his own manifestation. He enters a state technically known as *vismaya mudrā*, and is struck by peculiar experiences of a novel character flowing into his consciousness. These experiences are stages leading to union with the Supreme Being. This is known as *śāmbhava samāveśa*, and is characterized by mastery over the power of will. This is induced primarily by the grace of the Lord or by intense devotion or both. Human effort does not play much part in this. A mere hint or a reminder about God is enough to bring about such a situation. A mere talk of God, a sweet sound or a beautiful sight can send the recipient into the highest state of realization. Any words spoken about Kṛṣṇa brought tears into the eyes of Caitanya. When one day Maulānā Rūmi was passing by the shop of a goldsmith where three or four workers were beating sheets of gold the musical sound at once sent him into ecstasy which lasted for six hours. Closing his eyes he was singing all the time, "At the shop of a goldsmith I saw a brilliant vision of beauty—He in all His glory." His divine mood impressed the shop-keeper so much that in joy he distributed all his goods, and became his disciple. Paramahaṁsa Rāmakṛṣṇa, while still a boy, went into trance at the mere sight of a line of cranes flying in the sky, and fell unconscious in a field of paddy.

There are instances on record of great souls having been transported into ethereal heights of realization with no visible effort. Says the author, "Even without drinking the nectar of Thy devotion or even beholding Thee, creatures attain perfection by mere talk of Thee."[1] This form of *samāveśa* has always been coveted by aspirants through the ages. The author, who had already experienced the joy of *śākta samāveśa*, earnestly prayed for such an experience. He gave vent to his feelings thus, "Oh, when shall I, by virtue of sudden recognition, startle my master, the Lord, the one beyond fear, the magnanimous, the full, who has concealed His own form ?"[2] We come across numerous verses that give vent to the author's longing for such an experience, and we also have got evidence to believe that he did have such an experience in due time. His sense of fulfilment is borne out by his own sayings.

1. Verse 10/13 2. Verse 9/6.

A fine example of the sudden emergence of God consciousness is provided by the great Lalleśvarī of Kashmir, whose own words are of great relevance in this context. Says she, "I roared (like a river) at the source; irrigated the field with flood water. By the grace of that side (God) the world got awakened (yet) on my part I did not meditate on anything."[1]

In the case of *śākta samāveśa* supreme bliss follows realization, while in *śāmbhava samāveśa* realization comes in the wake of ecstasy. The distinctive features of the emergence of the two forms have been outlined by the author thus, "He alone has realized Thee, who is enraptured at Thy sight, or verily he, who has sudden ecstasy, has realized Thee."[2] In addition to the above *upāyas* there is a fourth one in which realization comes spontaneously with no effort. This is known as *anupāya* which is only a higher form of *śāmbhava samāveśa*. A devotee who has developed *Śiva* consciousness without any time-honoured disciplines is no other than *Śiva* Himself.

There are difficulties in the way of attempting to present a clear picture of the author's inner life. Since he has not chosen to write about himself, we have to be satisfied with what can be assembled from stray hints he has left behind. The narrative given here is solely based on what we have been able to glean out of his own sayings lying scattered throughout the book. It is not for an ordinary mortal to measure the greatness of a spiritual colossus that the author was. He was a veritable messenger from the Divine, who wandered here for a time in flesh and blood to remind us about our divine heritage, and returned to his divine abode after delivering his message.

1. Translation: Anand Kaul.
2. Verse 10/7.

ŚIVASTOTRĀVALĪ OF UTPALADEVA

Translation

Hymn No. 1

*All praise to the devotee, who, given neither to meditation nor to counting of beads, attains *Śiva* consciousness without any time-honoured means and without effort. (1)

**With accretions of dust gathered during the pilgrimage of life, my ātman, retaining all the youthfulness as a result of the immortal drink of Thy devotion, seems to be tarnished by grey hair. (2)

***The activities of devotees,who have found the wealth of Thy realization and dwell in Thy world, continue to be governed by the consummation of the same experience even during the course of worldly life. (3)

Lord, with the whole world conspicuously standing out as Thy being, what place therein is not sacred to the devotees and where does their *mantra* not bear fruit ? (4)

****Most exalted are those drunk with the bliss of the celestial wine of immortal devotion. They are rooted in non-dualism though having Thee, O Lord, as the second. (5)

---

*There are three *Upāyas* or means mentioned in *Śaiva* texts as leading to realization of *Śiva*. These are, *Āṇava*, *Śākta* and *Śāmbhava* corresponding to the physical, mental, and volitional aspects of man. But *Śiva* consciousness is attainable even without any spiritual effort as a matter of Divine grace. This is known as *Anupāya* or realization with no effort. Japa and other exercises are no condition for this exalted spiritual perfection. A person who has attained such a state is no other than *Śiva* Himself.

**The author admits in a figurative language that he had reached a stage of spiritual progress where he was able to take up worldly activities without losing his identity, though he appeared to the world outside as one influenced by it.

***Those who are well established in self-realization do not lose their awareness in mundane axistence.

****Bhakti* no doubt starts with a feeling of duality, but ends in complete coalescence with the object of worship.

Such persons alone, O Lord, as are steeped in the joy of intense devotion, know the very essence of Thy infinite ocean of bliss. (6)

*Thou art the self of all, and all are lovers of the self. Thus, attains excellence the man who knows Thy love as inhering in all. (7)

**Left alone, who may not cognize Thee, Lord, while the objective world remains dissolved (in *samādhi*)? To the devotees, however, Thou art clearly visible even during the interplay of the subject and the object. (8)

Let Thy love be inseparable from me in the same way as Thy dearest consort, the lake of infinite bliss, is from Thee. (9)

Lord, the course of sense perceptions, characterized by the triple sensations of pleasure, pain and delusion—all these are to the devotees but means to Thy attainment. (10)

***Master, devoid of the experience of the nectar of Thy love, even the advanced state of intellectual knowledge appears to me as sour as a ferment. (11)

****Those who have mastered the great science of Thy love are the only real knowers of the truth as regards both the pure and impure paths. (12)

**Bhakti* is not something to which we are total strangers. It is inherent in every being since everyone loves the Divinity of the self. What is needed is the understanding of a process consciously or unconsciously at work within our own being.

**There are two forms of *samādhi—nimīlana* and *unmīlana*. In the former a *yogī* is not aware of anything apart from his self as distinct from the body and other coverings while in the latter he views the whole world as his own self without losing his awareness. The author disparages the former as of no great significance as there is nothing to distract the *yogī* or disturb his poise. A devotee, on the other hand, maintains unmitigated awareness even during the interplay of the subject and the object.

***Knowledge without devotion is of no consequence, and connot lead to realization. In fact, devotion is the end of knowledge.

****There are seven states of experience right from *Śiva* to *Sakala*. The first four of these represent the pure path or the path of *vidyā*. They are *Śiva*, *Sadāśiva*, *Īśvara* and *Śuddha Vidyā* respectively. The impure path is represented by what are called *Vijñānākalas*, *Pralayākalas* and *Sakalas*. All these represent different layers of consciousness through which a *yogī* is to pass before attaining the highest state of *Śiva*.

*May the creeper of speech rising steadily from the root, saturated with the nectar of Thy love, bring forth copious fruit in the shape of ecstasy of love. (13)

"Becoming *Śiva* Himself, worship", thus goes the injunction. But, I say "Worship, after becoming a devotee". Thou art verily the Ultimate Reality discovered by devotees by unitive experience. (14)

What logic is not available to devotees to establish Thy oneness, and what the veils are not there for the vile to refute the same? (15)

**Lord, that Thou art attainable in a particular stage or a particular place by *yoga* is sheer humbug. Else, how art Thou visible to lovers in all states? (16)

The distinctive feature of lovers, not given to *pratyāhāra* and other practices, as against *yogīs*, is that they remain poised even in *vyutthāna*. (17)

Neither *yoga* nor austerities nor any other systen of worship is recommended. In this cult of *Śiva*, which recognizes no material means, *bhakti* alone is eulogized. (18)

***Ignorance having been dispelled by the light of love glowing within and without, let all determinate cognitions cease to the very name with all objects standing luminous in their true light. (19)

Oh, those devotees alone, on whose, tongue ever dwells the one word *Śiva*, experience the joy of all sense-objects put together. (20)

---

*Thought is inseparably connected with speech, which has four stages known as *parā*, *paśyantī*, *madhyamā* and *vaikharī*. As *parā* it germinally holds within it all knowledge, secular or spiritual besides all arts and sciences. It is also called *parā śakti* or *parā vāk*. The same knowledge materializes into *paśyantī*, where the words and their meaning are not distinguished as in the state of *Sadāśiva*. *Madhyamā* is the stage of the mind where the words and their meanings are differentiated from each other before passing on into the state of *vaikharī* or the articulate speech.

***Kuṇḍalinī yoga* like intellectual knowledge is of no avail unless based on *bhakti*. Devotees, however, behold the Lord in all His manifestations and in all conditions.

***The state of realization is technically known as Śri *Bhairavī mudrā*. In this state a *yogī* maintains awareness of his inner being with eyes wide open and without winking.

Whom else do they count—those who are comfortably seated in the transcendental bliss of the unruffled, cool, pure and sweet ocean of the nectar of love? (21)

Wherefore, O Lord, may not the sovereign remedy of Thy love be enjoyed by the like of me—a remedy whose natural corollary is what goes by the name of liberation ? (22)

Such fortunes alone are craved by good men as tend to strengthen the prospects of enjoying the sweetness of Thy love. (23)

The ineffable showers of the nectar of Thy love are experienced only by those, who, though fallen into the mire of attachment and aversion, are not affected thereby. (24)

What are spoken of as the fruits of *siddhis* starting with *aṇimā* and others and ending in liberation are simply inherent in the creeper of Thy love that has attained ripeness. (25)

Lord, how strange that the mind, which in essence is the seed of all suffering in the world, should bear the sublime fruit of liberation when imbued with the spirit of love. (26)

HYMN No. 2

Hail, O Conscious Principle, appearing variously in the shape of fire, Moon, Sun, *Brahmā*, *Viṣṇu*, the movable and the immovable. (1)

Hail to Thee, the Divine Fire (of knowledge) having the universe as the one oblation, and radiating pure effulgence after having smeared Thy body with the ashes of the universe converted into fuel. (2

Hail to Thee, O Soothing fire of *Śiva* brimming over with supreme immortality, the ineffable, exciting horror by the holocaust of the entire universe. (3)

I bow to Thee, O Supreme I-Consciousness, O *Mahādeva*, *Rudra*, *Śaṅkara*, *Śiva* and *Maheśvara*. (4)

Hail to the benevolent fire of *Śiva*, which, having completely consumed the three worlds, becomes terribly ablaze with the offering of their melting marrow. (5)

Hail to the sportful Lord, the mysterious *Śambhu*, whose only definition is the absence of all definability. (6)

Hail to the mysterious Lord, the antithesis of *Vedas* and *Āgamas*, all the same the author and the essence of the *Vedas* and *Āgamas*. (7)

Hail to Thee, O *Śambhu*, the only cause of the universe, the only destroyer, the immanent as also the transcendent. (8)

Hail to the *Śambhu*, the full, the root, the middle and the end, the conglomerate of the root, the middle and the end, yet devoid of the root, the middle and the end. (9)

Hail to Thee, O *Śiva*, difficult of attainment, a single utterance of whose name is the outcome of a heap of merits. (10)

I bow to Thee alone, O Conscious Principle, the bearer of skulls, having assumed the form of the movable and the immovable, ever sporting with hordes of realized beings. (11)

Hail to the miraculous *Śambhu*, the juggler, the pure, the unmanifest, the manifest, the subtle and of the form of the universe. (12)

Hail to Thee, O worker of miracles, the omnipotent, having as Thy sport the dissolution of the universe, the creation of *Brahmā*, *Viṣṇu* and *Indra*. (13)

Hail to Thee, O fathomless ocean of *Hara*, even the strayers on whose shores achieve all sorts of powers. (14)

Hail to the exquisite lotus of *Śambhu*, living untainted in the thick mire of the material world. (15)

Hail to Thee, the most exalted, the good, the pure, the fountain-head, the ornament, the dearest and the Ultimate Reality. (16)

Hail to the indefinable *Śambhu*, ever bound, yet enjoying eternal liberation, the one beyond bondage and liberation. (17)

In all this threefold world—a mere hoax in essence—I bow to Thee alone, O one without a second, resting in eternal bliss, (18)

Hail to Thee, O *Śarva*, the essence of the right order, the lover of the left order, having all orders as Thy own and yet without an order. (19)

Hail to Thee, adorable in any manner, worshiped in any place whatsoever, to him, whatever the *Deva*. (20)

Hail to Thee, O giver of boons, the goal of the seekers of liberation, the remover of all afflictions, an infinite expanse of beauty. (21)

Hail to Thee, O Master, the ever full, filling the whole of the three worlds with the sweetness of endless bliss. (22)

Hail to Thee, the fearsome conglomerate of *Śaktis* that worship Thee through the enjoyment of pleasure giving sense objects. (23)

Hail to Thee, the ineffable something, not accessible even to *munis*, yet hugged by those, whose movements are prompted by devotion. (24)

Hail to Thee, the treasure-house of supreme immortality, the heap of supreme immortality, attainable high above the highest of states. (25)

I bow to that stainless and soothing form of Universal Consciousness, alluring on account of matchless fragrance and abounding in the joy of supreme immortality. (26)

*On the infinite tablet of Thy unitive experience, brimming over with the nectar of freedom, I bow, O Lord, to that philosophy of Thine which knows no script whatsoever. (27)

We bow to that cult of *Maheśvara*, the destroyer of all fear, the remover of adversity and the consumer of all that is inauspicious. (28)

Adoration, adoration to Thee, O *Deva*, The whole universe is resting on Thee. Thou art the Supreme Lord of the worlds. Isolated from Thee, I come to Thee for refuge. (29)

HYMN NO. 3

Adoration to the miraculous *Śambhu*, who as the third transcends the twofold aspect of the objective world—the real and the unreal. (1)

---

*Knowledge of the self is a super-conscious experience not to be acquired from books. It is the direct outcome of *samādhi* and not a subject of philosophical speculation.

Right from *devarṣis* downwards in this threefold world of bondage they alone are free, who are devoted to Thee, the Free. (2)

They alone are resting in peace to whom the constant remembrance of Thy cosmic form constitutes the only panacea for the ills of the world. (3)

Whose white canopy is the self-illumined moon, whose fan is the stream of heaven—he alone is the Lord Supreme. (4)

Luminous, cooling and pure as the digit of the moon, cast Thou on me, O Lord, a single glance overflowing with ineffable immortality. (5)

Wherefore may not these drops of knowledge fallen from Thy ocean of consciousness and bliss, O Lord, savour of immortal sweetness ? (6)

Lord, they are heartless indeed, whose hearts are not immersed in the ecstasy of Thy love. In fact, they are despicable. (7)

He alone, whose heart has become merged in Thee, the Lord, is eligible for Lordlike powers. (8)

The immortal stream of Thy contemplation simultaneously washes away all sense of exultation and grief just as low and high places are made even by inundation. (9)

What state of theirs should not overflow with joy, who, O Lord, under no circumstances part with Thee as dearer than self. (10)

*I roar and, lo, I dance. My dream has come true having come across Thee, my Lord of exquisite beauty. (11)

---

*According to the commentator the verse signifies the author's entrance into what is known as *vismaya mudrā*, which is a prelude to the attainment of a high state of realization. It highlights the state of a seeker, who is stunned to find his fond dream materialize all of a sudden, and becomes maddened with the bliss of devotion on recognizing his master as possessed of exquisite beauty. When this type of devotion awakens in the heart of an aspirant, his behaviour becomes erratic. Like a mad man he often laughs, dances, roars, sings or weeps for no apparent reason. We have got numerous examples of *mahātmās* having passed through such an experience. In recent times *Svāmī Muktānanda* of Ganeshpuri passed through such a state. Says he, "I roared so much that the cows nearby broke their ropes and ran helter skelter, dogs barked madly and people rushed to my hut ... Sometimes I would zig zag along the ground like a snake, sometimes hop like a frog, sometimes roar like a tiger "(Svāmī Muktānanda: *Cit Śakti Vilas*, p. 116). What is stated here is not a poetic exaggeration but a fact which is literally true.

(THIS IS A STATE) Where nothing remains to be known, nothing to be done, no other *yoga* nor any perceptivity; what knowledge remains is the offering of the universe to be consumed in the fire of pure consciousness which reigns supreme. (12)

They have secured instant release from the tentacles of pain, invincible and endless—those whose speech ever resounds with the sound *Śiva*. (13)

The first person (I) is distinct from the second (You) and the third (He) persons. Thou art the one great person, the prop of all persons. (14)

Most exalted are those world-honoured votaries of Thine, O Lord of the universe, to whom this very ocean of the world constitutes a vast swimming pool. (15)

*Leave alone other entreaties of Thy votaries; in this cult of *Śiva*, they feel shy even to implore Thee to reveal Thyself. (16)

"Above Me there is naught, yet I perform *Japa*. Real *Japa* is the consciousness of identity"—this Thou enjoineth by the rosary in some of Thy forms. (17)

The unreal is different from the real, O Lord, and so is the real from the unreal. Thou art different from the unreal as also from the real, and art, therefore, of the nature of both the real and the unreal. (18)

Having light brighter than the beams of thousands of suns, and though pervading the entire universe, Thou still art not visible.(19)

Thou art sentience in the insentient, and verily the knower of the knowable. Pervading the limited world, Thou art the highest of all. (20)

Enough of other Lamentations. Only this much I shout hoarse before the Lord :—"O Master, I get deluded even after knowing Thee" (21)

---

*The other entreaties alluded to are those for super-natural powers. When a *yogī* transcends the ordinary mind certain higher powers come to him unsought in accordance with the laws of the spiritual world. They are considered as obstacles in the path and small-minded *sādhakas* are likely to be allured by them. True *sādhakas* use them with great caution as they impede spiritual progress. One must steer clear of them and concentrate on the final goal. Devotees do not want anything apart from the lotus feet of the Lord.

HYMN No. 4

Though capricious, O Mind, thou art, nevertheless, praiseworthy, devoted as thou art to the refuge even of the Lords of creation, the precepter of the three worlds, the consort of the Supreme Mother. (1)

*Having scaled the succession of the rungs of the ladder of various divinities, even holding fast to the adorable feet of *Śiva*, Oh, I still do not part with the lower plane. (2)

Reveal, O Lord, Thy path and suspend all my mundane activities so that I may forthwith become an ever-alert servant of Thine. (3)

O *Śiva*, O *Śiva*, O *Śambhu*, O *Śaṅkara*, O lover of Thy devotees, quicken Thy grace. He who has set himself to the contemplation of Thy pair of lotus feet has salvation not far off. (4)

Those clung to the stool of Thy lotus feet create worlds of their own choice. They mock at the Lord of creation as one having become tainted with the bonds of authority, bereft of all freedom. (5)

**But for Thy luminous form nothing is capable of being perceived. Thus, though veiled by nature, Thou, O Lord, art ever within sight. (6)

Some taste the nectar of Thy lotus feet with attitudes vitiated by dualism; others taste of Thee as ever manifest, of undiminished glory, devoid of duality. (7)

Lord, Thy vision, which comes to me off and on like a flash of lightning, steeped in immortal bliss—should it come to stay, Thou wouldst be rightly worshipped. What else should I need? (8)

*The various rungs of the ladder of divinities represent successive layers of consciousness corresponding to the states of *Brahmā*, *Viṣṇu*, *Rudra*, *Īśvara* and *Sadāśiva* through which a *yogī* is expected to pass before touching the state of *Śiva*. What the verse seems to stress is how powerful the lower nature is so as to be able to pull one down from the highest state of realization. One must, therefore, maintain strict vigil till all forces of lower nature are subdued and perfect freedom acheived.

**It is the light of consciousness that holds together both the object and the cognizing subject. The very act of cognition implies some sort of kinship between the subject and the object. According to the author all that exists is light. Nothing can exist outside this. For a fuller discussion see Introduction pp. 45-46.

Thou art all; alien there is naught—real or unreal. Just as Thy reality is determined here thus by higher wisdom, the same way be Thou manifest to me with no effort in all states. (9)

At Thy own bidding, O Lord, hast Thou made me set foot on Thy path; wherefore then do I behave like common folk, knowing nothing worthy of Thy sublime state ? (10)

What a sweet and lofty emotion of love for Thee, O Lord, blossoms in their hearts, in the wake of which they—the *cātakas* looking wistfully to the thunder of Thy praises—become graced with protracted communion. (11)

By what scheme of Thine has this uncommon love for Thee ripened in Thy votaries so that a mere mention or a reminder in the state of separation begets the joy of a tryst ? (12)

Exalted are they whose mouth ever rings with the sound *Śiva*, showering sweet, sublime nectar like the moon emerging from the abode of nectar. Nourished with the spirit of transcendent ecstasy, the word *Śaṅkara* repeated a hundred times inspires even the bosoms of animals with ever new savours. (13/14)

*This fearful world has well-nigh come to an end; the heavy dross of the mind has melted away; still there is, O Lord, not the least opening in the bolted panels of Thy city gates. (15)

With heart pining to behold the core of the ever blooming lotus of Thy countenance, deign, O Lord, to appear face to face before me. (16)

Is there a joy or power on earth greater than the sense of oneness with Thee ? Wherefore, then doth the mind of Thy devotees stray into wrong channels abandoning all that ? (17)

Should I not be constantly sipping with love the wine of harmony with Thee, for a moment shall I not be a fit receptacle for Thy realization. (18)

Sullied by sense of duality, man certainly does not behold Thy true form. Nevertheless, omniscient and lover of Thy devotees as Thou art, wherefore dost Thou not lend ear to this wailing of mine ? (19)

---

*The verse is suggestive of what is known in mystic circles as *śūnya bhūmī*. It is a negative experience and must be overcome with relentless effort combined with the Lord's grace.

Lord, dost Thou remember if ever I strove or prayed for sense-enjoyment ? Uninterrupted vision of Thy immortal form is enough. Pray, give me that. (20)

Great Lord, the moment I set foot on Thy path at Thine own pleasure, all blessedness dawned on me there and then. What else may I ask of Thee ? (21)

*Where the sun, the moon and other luminaries set—blessed is that ineffable night of *Śiva*, shining with the exuberance of its own light. (22)

Destitute of the immortal sweetness of the touch of Thy feet, the acquirement of the overlordship of the three worlds, O Lord of the immortals, holds out no charm for me. (23)

This knot of the self, O Lord, tied only by Thee to conceal Thy form is so tight that ignoring Thee, visible to me (in *samādhi*) it does not relent a bit on the physical plane. (24)

To great ones, O Lord of the immortals, though the object of worship, Thou constantly stayeth as the worshipper. Visible within and without, Thou eternally shineth as the seer. (25)

HYMN No. 5

**As one whose only interest lies in the contact of Thy lotus feet, seize me by the collar, O Lord, and hurl me into Thy abode. (1)

**Śiva's* night is the high state of realization in which the world of relativity fades into oblivion while the *yogī* remains fully conscious of his identity. It is a self-lumious state not depending on any external source of light such as the sun, the moon or other l uminaries which o we their luminosity to the light of consciousness. Says the *Śvetāśvataropaniṣad*, "The sun does not shine there, neither the moon nor the stars. These lightnings do not shine there—how then this fire? Because He shines, everything shines after Him. By His light a ll this shines" (6/14). The same idea is re-echoed in the *Bhagavadgīta*, "The sun does not illumine that, nor the moon nor fire; having attained which men do not return into transmigratory existence —that is my supreme state" (15/6).

**Here the author gives vent to his longing for that vehement form of divine grace which is technically known as *haṭha Śaktipāta*. This is an extraordinary phenomenon which does not admit of any explanation.

With the hair of my crown glistening with heaps of dust fallen from Thy lotus feet, when shall I with extreme vehemence start to be a dancer? (2)

Lord, with Thee as the one master, this much I pray that dwelling within Thee I would better be speechless than a wise man otherwise. (3)

O Lord, O Fountain-head of immortality, O bliss absolute, O three-eyed, O sweetness absolute, O fearful-eyed,— thus shouting, Oh, would I dance ! (4)

The eyes having got closed at the touch of Thy lotus feet, let me dance, reeling under the intoxication of the wine of Thy love. (5)

Lord, let me reside in a particular recess of the mountain of the mind, where lies the supreme joy of unbroken state of Thy contemplation. (6)

*Where Thou along with Thy consort stayeth in Thy manifold form, from the mansion-house right upto the city gates—of that sanctuary of Thine, Oh, would I become a denizen ! (7)

Let Thy sun-beams, O Lord, radiate in full so that the lotus of my heart bursts open for Thy worship. (8)

Grant, O Lord, that staggering on Thy path my mind, having tasted ever new states, gets wild with excitement or even liquidated. (9)

Reveal Thyself, O Lord, out of pleasure or pain, from within a pillar or even a pitcher, out of external objects or from within (10)

Let the extremely soothing nectar of the touch of Thy lotus feet flow in an unbroken current within and without and for all time. (11)

Drowned in the immortal lake of the touch of Thy lotus feet, let me for all time enjoy that ineffable bliss that surpasses all other enjoyments. (12)

Accept, O Lord, all attachment and aversion consecrated by me. Having received and divinized them partake of these along with Thy devotees. (13)

Ever content with the food of the whole universe as Thou art,

*The mansion-house represents the world of consciousness. The city gates are the senses whose field of operation is the world outside.

grant Thy votaries, O Lord, an opportunity of Thy glance of grace that they might rest in peace. (14)

With eyes not closed having tasted the joy of inner love, let me worship even pieces of straw as, "Prostration to *Śivā*, my own self." (15)

Even after having attained union with Thee, realizing the universe as my own glory, let me not part with the joy of the spirit of devotion. (16)

With naught else to be desired, being without a second, what is known as Thy fullness is perfectly tenable. (17)

Where one laughs and dances, where attraction and repulsion are eaten up, where the sweet nectar of immortal love is given to drink—that state, Oh, would I attain. (18)

Let the highly rapturous aroma of the flower of Thy remembrance come to stay in my mind so that the stench of foul impressions is wiped away. (19)

What comparison is there between attachment for sense-objects and devotion to the lotus feet of *Hara* ? Thus, O Immortal, apprise my mind of contradictory tastes as to what is really beneficial. (20)

Even passing through the stages of *yoga*, though given to withdrawal of senses from their objects, I would fain have a restless mind, drunk with the vintage of Thy love. (21)

On the plane of speech, in the various states of the mind and in bodily movements through the organs, in all places and at all times, let the bliss of love be my constant companion. (22)

"*Śiva, Śiva, Śiva*"—constantly repeating this Thy name, let me, O Lord. remain tasting that sublime joy, which has not known any recounting. (23)

The entire world of matter having been destroyed, let me traverse the infinite and effulgent universe of consciousness, which admits of no other conscious compartment, all the same worshipping Thee. (24)

Nothing is of avail for getting established in one's own self, conspicuously luminous and immortal. Let this lofty conviction strike firm roots in me, having been purified by the dust of Thy lotus feet. (25)

At times, O Lord, something super-normal flashes in the hearts of those who have touched the soles of Thy feet, in which experience all this universe melts away in the ocean of immortality. Do give me that for all time to come. (26)

HYMN No. 6

*To one burning with a moment's separation from Thee, Lord, be Thou ever the cynosure of my sight. (1)

**In this cycle of transmigration, characterized by separation, O Lord, Let me ever remain united with Thee, my beloved, while actively associated with the world. (2)

Whatever I experience through the body, the speech and the mind all that art Thou—though the supreme truth, let this become a constant fact of experience with me. (3)

Just as Thou art indeterminate consciousness and full of supreme bliss, let my speech ever singing of Thee, also become like that. (4)

*Cases are on record of persons having high fever in the heat of devotion.

It is said that Amir Khusro lost his mother in his early life, and was, therefore, brought up by his father. When the boy woke up in the morning and his father changed his shirt, it was found to have been scorched at the portion that covered his chest.

During the course of his *sādhanā*, Paramahaṁsa Rāmakṛṣṇa was found at one time to have been running high fever. Several doctors were called in but no one was able to bring his temperature down. At last, a yoginī, who happened to be there at the time came, and, after examining the Paramahaṁsa declared that he was passing through a stage of *sādhanā* known as *mahā bhāva* which was responsible for the fever. She said that it was not a physiological case and that no amount of medication would help. To prove her point she asked them to prepare sandal paste and apply it on his body. As soon as this was done his temperature returned to normal. The author's assertion that he was burning with a moment's separation from the Lord can, therefore, be taken as literally true.

**The word *viyojitaḥ* in the second line of the verse is ambiguous, and may be interpreted to mean either as separated or as actively associated. In the former case the word *api* becomes superfluous. We have, therefore, adopted the latter interpretation. which is in keeping with the author's philosophy of cultivating self-awareness in the midst of active worldly life.

At Thy own inspiration beholding all objects as Thyself, let me wander about with no desire, full of exultation. (5)

Lord, how would I behold the entire universe as filled with Thee ! With this much only shall I become contented, and Thou wilt not be pestered thereafter. (6)

Let all objects, steadily losing their impurities, ever appear to me as merging in Thee like flecks of clouds in the firmament. (7)

From within the universe, let Thy ineffable jewel, that dispels the endless chain of darkness by its scintillating lustre become visible to me in all states. (8)

What state dost Thou not pervade ? What object is there that is not Thy being? Wearied that I am now, let me without effort realize Thee on all sides. (9)

*Let the bliss of clasping Thy form come to me at will. Having attained this, say, O Lord, what have I not gained ? (10)

Reveal Thyself—by no other entreaty do we disturb Thee. Smarting with separation, we seek Thee and Thee alone. (11)

HYMN No. 7

Having attained harmony with Thee, the ocean of bliss, Lord, let my mind once for all give up all this sorry scheme of things dominated by disharmony. (1)

Let the axe of realization of oneness with Thee fall on the trammels of attachment, aversion and others which have become deep rooted as 'This is mine, not that'. (2)

Lord, let the chain of stigmas of delusion melt away and perfect freedom flash forth in my heart. Let my conscious being become suffused with the nectar of bliss. (3)

Suffocating within the egg-shell of the world formed of attachment and others, let the mother of Thy devotion nourish me with all sweet essences that I may grow wings and become a denizen of heavens. (4)

*The reference is to *śāmbhava samāveśa* which is characterized by mastery over will power. This is the highest state of realization, having attained which nothing more remains to be sought.

Let this mind of mine acquire the skill of imbibing the immortal essence of the sweetness of love for Thy feet till the tendency towards the poison of sense-objects is eradicated. (5)

At the touch of the sun-beams of Thy love, let this mind-jewel of mine once for all shoot out the blazing sparks of attachment and others. (6)

In that surpassingly high state, where even *Hari*, *Indra* and *Brahmā* keep waiting outside, Oh, would I for ever sing aloud of Thee. (7)

As an outcome of wild excitement caused by the ecstasy of love, let me through the senses perceive the whole world absolutely us *Śiva* and all actions as constituting worship. (8)

*Let my mind, having taken Thy devotion for a spouse of high birth bear aṇimā and others as sons and let her become deep-rooted with the firm attachment that "All these are mine". (9)

HYMN No. 8.

**The scantling of grace vested in the Lord and the semblance of devotion devolved on me, when shall the two hand in hand converge into that super-conscious state ? (1)

Begotten through constant enjoyment of Thy Mastership, let the one ineffable bliss of fulfilment dawn within me for all time in this very world. Away with the eminent states of knowledge, *Yoga* and others. (2)

Like common folk, O Lord, may I have increased infatuation for sense-objects. Only would I behold them as Thy being having lost all sense of differentiation. (3)

In the different states of the body, in the modifications of the mind, in the course of the vital airs and in different sense-perceptions into which Thou hast become differentiated, be Thou conspicuous to me in Thy own ineffable being. (4)

Let these sense-faculties of mine delightfully fall on their respective objects, yet, not for a moment, O Lord, may I run the

*Vide note on verse 9/18.

**Divine grace and human effort are interlinked, each dependent on the other. Both are essential for spiritual perfection. It is God who attracts; *bhakti* is the soul's response to it.

slightest risk of parting with the bliss of harmony with Thee. (5)

At Thy inspiration let me rise above all worldy transactions viewing the multitude of objects as light, tender, bright, clear and soothing in essence. (6)

Let my being blossom into Thyself; let all worlds come to be my own limbs and let all this world, the outcome of duality, pass into oblivion even after entering the realm of memory. (7)

Let there well up such a deluge of the sublime nectar of the vision of Thy visage that the dark abyss obscuring my realization of oneness with Thee is filled to the brim. (8)

Should I ever get moistened with a tiny drop of the nectar of Thy communion, I shall not turn my back on worldly pleasures, having been stripped of the sense of duality. (9)

*On top, at the root or in the middle, O Unborn, let the nelumbo stem of Thy devotion be ever accessible to me, the holy swan ever gliding on the lotus lake of Thy feet. (10)

Lord, let all things approach me either as objects of thought or of sight. Only let them shine before my sight and thought as the embodiment of supreme immortal light. (11)

Great Lord, in all predicaments facing me let me not only grow fearless, but also have boundless exultation at the touch of Thy body. (12)

The whole universe threaded into Thy being is also projected as outside Thee—let this understanding cultivated by me with firm determination become a fact of experience even on the physical plane. (13)

HYMN No. 9

**When shall my mind, pining for ever new experiences of joy, become engaged in Thy touch, having given up all else ?(1)

When shall this aspirant, solely committed to Thee, having as his valuable asset the mere worship of Thy feet, directly realize Thee ? (2)

*Nelumbo stem is found in lotus ponds and lakes everywhere. In Kashmir it is considered a prize vegetable known as *nadru*.

**There are three stages of realization, *Dhyāna, darśana* and *sparśa*. The first is the attempt at concentration, and the second, the actual experience of the Divine. The third is the struggle to hold fast to it.

Under the spell of intense love, when shall my mind, having become unmindful of everything, and with a bang breaking asunder all strong door pins, step into Thy presence ? (3)

Lord, when shall I, by dint of Thy love, subjugate the sense deities seated in the heart, the seat of consciousness ? (4)

Lord, when shall I have in abundant measure the ecstasy of love, as an outcome of which the objective world, though bearing distinct names, is filled with the bliss of consciousness? (5)

*When shall I, by virtue of sudden recognition, startle my master, the Lord, the one beyond fear, the magnanimous, the full, the causeless, who has veiled His own self ? (6)

Lord, when shall I become a fit receptacle for Thy grace as a result of which it may not be worthy of Thee to steal away from me ? (7)

**Viewing all sentient beings as essentially engaged in Thy worship, when shall I, through the same vision, become fully saturated with the bliss of love ? (8)

Lord, when shall my yearning for Thy love—the highest state of knowledge and the highest stage of yoga—attain fulfilment ? (9)

When shall I, in the height of exultation, reveal to all the treasure of Thy holy feet, suddenly obtained and firmly grasped ? (10)

Lord, when shall I become one with Thy light of consciousness radiating on all sides, so that not a trace of darkness of *Māyā* is left in me ? (11)

Having assimilated the whole universe into myself, when shall I, O Lord, become dispassionate, the doyen of the community of Thy devotees ? (12)

Lord, Thou art the unique cause of all egos; when shall I have

*Sudden recognition implies *Śāmbhava* form of *samāveśa*, which is a product of divine grace. For further elucidation see Introduction.

**The universe is not a product of *avidyā*. There is a definite plan behind it drawn meticulously by a conscious being. Everything has a divine purpose and everyone a part to play. It is not for man to move away from the scheme of things. Co-operation with the scheme of nature is the real worship.

Universal I-consciousness, brimming over with the spirit of love ? (13)

Firmly clasping the goddess of devotion, enveloping all objects, when shall I relax peacefully in the soothing pair of the lotuses of Thy feet ? (14)

When shall I reach the height of the wealth of Thy joyous worship, reinforced with the wine of love and become fulfilled ? (15)

*With the voice choked by streaming tears of ecstasy—bewildered and stammering—and face flushed with laughter, when shall I receive Thy soothing touch ? (16)

Having shaken off this state, virtually resembling that of animals, when shall I, O Lord, find myself as worthy of Thy lovers ? (17)

***Aṇimā* and other *siddhis* having been attained, all fear of calamities having been warded off, when shall I become established in the sport of drinking the invigorating elixir of Thy love ? (18)

Lord, when shall my speech pronounce such a lament in the wake of which, Thy form flashes forth suddenly before my eyes ? (19)

With heart tuned to the pursuit of firmly clasping Thy lotus feet, when shall I with no effort clearly behold Thee as all this—real as also unreal ? (20)

HYMN No. 10

Verily, this should not be tolerable by Thee, the one master of the universe that those who have acquired universal conscious-

*The verse highlights the impact of super-conscious experience on the body during the initial stages of *sādhanā*. The body must be pure and strong enough to bear the shock.

**These are the eight *siddhis* mentioned by Patañjali in his *Yoga Sūtras*. They are (1) *aṇimā* (becoming as subtle as an atom), (2) *mahimā* (becoming as big as the biggest thing on earth), (3) *garimā* (becoming heavy at will), (4) *laghimā* (becoming light at will), (5) *prāpti* (capacity to touch the farthest point), (6) *prākāmya* (power to get things done at will), (7) *Iśitva* (Lordship over all), and (8) *vaśitva* (control over all). These powers appear unsought in the advanced stages of *sādhanā*. They are considered obstacles as they are likely to tempt aspirants and deflect them from the right path. Genuine *sādhakas*, however, do not attach much importance to them, and use them with utmost caution without getting attached in any way.

ness should at the same time behave like common folk (in *vyutthāna*). (1)

Those who at all times lovingly follow Thy footsteps enjoy supersensuous bliss wherever they go. (2)

Whence the disease where Thou, the destroyer of death, is the protector ? What craving for other enjoyments is there where the light of non-dualism reigns supreme ? (3)

He who has discovered Thee, the all-pervading Lord even by a moment's experience of joy, has all his time there and then filled with Thy bliss. (4)

The moon is but a drop of nectar of Thy bliss fallen on the world. Likewise, is the sun but a ray of Thy consuming light. Let me be consecrated, O Lord, to Thy third eye, the one symbol of indefinable, transcendental glory. (5/6)

*He alone has seen Thee, who becomes enraptured at Thy sight, or he who somehow has abrupt experience of ineffable ecstasy, has seen Thee. (7)

Lord, those on whom descends Thy grace, who have unravelled Thy essence, having drawn out the external world from Thy fulness, they have again merged the same into the inner being.(8)

Sans Thee, the whole world is seen as having even (two) eyes, while Thou, its one Lord, has odd (three) eyes. (9)

That nihilists have no existence apart from Thee, leave alone this fact; even the talk of Thy negation is not tenable without Thee. (10)

Lord, shouldst Thou be enshrined in my heart secure from the chain of external and internal impediments, what else is of avail ? (11)

Some move, O Lord, from birth to birth extremely unsettled in themselves; others, O Lord, move about joyously poised in themselves. (12)

**Even without drinking the nectar of Thy devotion or even beholding Thee creatures attain perfection by mere talk of Thee. (13)

*The verse alludes to the two forms of *samāveśa, śāmbhava* and *śākta*. In the former case realization is preceded by ecstasy while in the latter it comes in the wake of it.

**There are some gifted souls blessed with a sharp memory and a mind free from *vāsanās* either as a result of good deeds performed in previous

Lord, we are Thy servants, and as such entitled to Thy full care in the same way as Thou sustaineth the three worlds. (14)

*Even though I have realized Thy immanent form of immortal bliss, still I am extremely pining for the joy of Thy touch. (15)

O *Deva*, all afflictions suffered by men of the world become tolerable when associated with what is known as Thy aspect of *dhṛti*. (16)

Lord, with Thee existing as the conscious principle, omniscient and omnipotent, the manifestation of the world, though shadowy, is understandable. (17)

Animated by Thee, these senses, though insentient like a lump of clay, pulsate with life and dance like flakes of cotton carried away by the wind. Shouldst these senses not be possessed of self-consciousness, who, O Lord, would stop the realization of the universe as one with Thee ? (18-19)

Great Lord, those great ones are also adorable, who, though gone to dissolution, are yet purified by the touch of the fire of Thy fury. (20)

With Thee manifestly obtaining on all sides in Thy form of supreme light, wherefore, O Lord, do I stray in darkness ? (21)

My immortal self is Thy indivisible being; yet I am the abode of nothing but mortal characteristics. (22)

He alone is exalted, whose speech is adorned with the name of *Maheśvara*, and whose forehead bears the mark of prostration. (23)

Lord, wherefore does not realization come to me spontaneously with no effort since Thou art both the real and the unreal ? (24)

What happiness is there not attainable by a devotee of *Śiva*, one dwelling in unity with *Śiva* ? As such I am propitiable even by heads of *devas* with the wine of immortality. (25)

Seated midway between the navel and the heart of animate beings, in the form of gastric heat, Thou consumeth, O Great Fire, all that moves and moves not. (26)

births or due to single-minded devotion to God or both. They are so sensitive that a mere talk of God is enough to send them into *samādhi*. For further information see Introduction.

*Vide note on verse 9/1.

HYMN No. 11

Neither the world is mine, nor a friend, nor even a kinsman : with Thyself as all this, who need be alien to me ? (1)

Master, Thou art the Lord Supreme; the whole universe is naught else but Thee. May this truth become a fact of realization —even this entreaty is after all an entreaty. (2)

Inasmuch as the Lordship of the three worlds appears here as a piece of straw to those given to Thee, what other fruit than Thy remembrance will their good deeds bear? (3)

Since nothing is different from Thee, even the lords of the universe being Thy manifestation, Thy miraculous acts do not admit of any praise. (4)

*One with Thee am I, constantly given to Thy worship. Though ceaselessly meditating thus, wherefore, O Lord, do I not involuntarily maintain the same poise even in the state of dream? (5)

Those who are blessed with just a trail of the aroma of Thy lotus feet, to them all objects of enjoyment, coveted even by gods, appear stinking. (6)

**Thou dost not vary in Thy heart, the speech or action, O *Śambhu*. What is required to be bestowed on one basically guileless is one thing out of the two—grace or otherwise. (7)

Ignorant am I, woe-stricken, scared by old age and other maladies. Being powerless, I have taken refuge in Thee. Deign, O Lord, that I may ere long attain the highest of all states, past the path of pain. (8)

***Having reached Thy ears, my laments, though meagre, fetch the highest price just as drops of rain fallen within the core of the bamboo become precious pearls. (9)

*The author had already realized his identity in the wakeful state and was now out to carry the thread of awareness into the other two states of dream and deep sleep.

**A *mahātmā* as defined in the *śāstras* is one who is one in thought, word and deed. Since the Lord is the true *mahātmā*, it is but meet that He should confer on His devotees one thing out of the two—grace or otherwise—and not one thing in *samāveśa* and quite the opposite in *vyutthāna*.

***There is an old fable that drops of rain fallen within the core of a bamboo tree during a particular position of stars are converted into *vaṃsalocana* which is of great medicinal value.

Oh, what is not attained even by those who even for a moment feign to be intent on Thy name ? O bearer of the crescent on Thy head, grant that conquering death, I may attain *aṇimā* and other powers. (10)

O *Śambhu*, O *Śarva*, O *Śiva*, the bearer of the crescent on Thy head, O three-eyed, the bearer of rosary, O blessed one, shining with Thy symbol of awe-inspiring skulls, having the fearful trident as Thy weapon, O ocean of mercy, given to the creation of the three worlds, the embodiment of terrible power, O *Śrīkaṇṭha*, liquidate the stock of all evil and grant highest perfection. (11)

What is there of which, O Master, the Lord is not the author ? What state of the sentient beings is that not controlled by *Śaṅkara* ? Thus, though ever depending on Thee, the great Lord of unmitigated glory, constantly stricken with anguish, I experience in this world naught but suffering. (12)

In this world, O giver of boons, even though disease, old age and death have the upper hand, yet, leaving these alone for a while, even the much-coveted sound and other sense-objects are fleeting. Even then, as a seeker of abiding peace, I yearn for the enduring, sublime elixir of life characterized by sweet meditation on Thy lotus feet. (13)

O Lord, adept in removing the distress of Thy votaries, O treasure-house of happiness, having *Gaṅgā* in Thy tuft of hair, grant that I, the abode of mere pain, scared by birth and death may, while still alive, engaged in Thy worship, enjoy enduring, sublime powers, yielding unmitigated bliss even from sense-objects. (14)

Adoration to Him, whose only activity is the destruction of the blinding darkness of delusion, whose light surpasses all other lights and whose emblem is the moon. (15)

HYMN No. 12

No helping hand is called for, since there is nothing to thwart Thy vision. By Thee alone is all this pervaded. Wherefore then art Thou not visible even now ? (1)

Manifesting from the multitude of objects, from within the various senses, from knowledge itself, Oh, would I spontaneously behold the Lord for all time and in all quarters having overcome all sense of relativity. (2)

How can they re-incarnate, and endowed with what characteristic nature, wilt they come into limelight—those whom lifting miraculously from land, water, straw and what not, Thou saturateth with immortal streams of realization ? (3)

Satiated with the nectar flowing from direct realization of Thy being, having eradicated desire, the inebriates wander at their will. (4)

*Neither always nor then nor once—where no such notion of time exists, that is Thy realization. This cannot be termed as eternal or otherwise. (5)

With the mind set upon Thy vision, let me have this much only as the fruit of *yoga* that by the mere wish I may gain entrance into Thy sanctuary of immortality for the purpose of Thy worship. (6)

With mind abloom following the attainment of Thy absolute realization, the selfless movements and saying of *mahātmās* come into prominence as a mere sport. (7)

Dwelling within Thy feet, Lord, let me, with movements not fettered, adore my master fearlessly in all stages of mundane life. (8)

Having become merged in the core of Thy lotus feet, all desires having subsided, let me move about at will fully satiated with the honey of super-sensuous bliss. (9)

Appropriate realization dawns on him too in whom the idea of Thy worship has emanated even pretentiously. (10)

Indifferent to all else, Oh, shall I, with mind extremely equipoised, drink of the Lord to the fill, O Master, easy of attainment, being omnipresent. (11)

Divorced from Thee, all this is worthy of dismissal; viewed as Thyself, the same is worthy of acceptance—this, in short, is the substance of all wisdom. (12)

*Realization connotes loss of temporal and spatial conceptions. In such a state the words always , then or once become meaningless. Even the words eternal or otherwise are inapplicable.

The objective world, viewed as existing within Thee, is eminently adorable as the Lord Himself; apart from Thee, Lord, how can non-existence be conceived of, much less adored? (13)

*Transcending speech and determinate knowledge, let me, O Three Eyed Lord, objectively cognize Thee and Thee alone everywhere without obstacles even during the confusion of the subject and the object. (14)

Unveil, O *Deva*, Thy abode, in which Thou stayeth with the supreme mistress. Those who have become one with the dust of the Master's feet—do they merit distrust ? (15)

**Even after having come within my ken, wherefore dost Thou O Lord, elude me, Thy servant ? To what creature dost Thou not form a moment's object of sight ? (16)

Saturated with perennially flowing crystalline streams of the nectar of unitive experience, when shall I, my Lord, bring myself into absolute oneness with Thee and attain bliss ? (17)

Let me have just an iota of Thy sublime self-consciousness, which envelopes the whole universe as I and thereby become Thy worshipper. (18)

Every moment, while beholding different objects, Oh, would I, with no effort experience nothing but Thee, my Master of unlimited form as having assumed the form of the universe. (19)

***Wherefore dost not the mind pursue different objects of desire as constituting Thy body ? In this way it will not suffer loss of nature while my highest dream will also attain realization. (20)

*The verse refers to what is known as *unmīlana samādhi* in which a *yogī* realizes the world outside as *Śiva* identical with one's own self. In the first lap of sādhanā a seeker realizes his own self as distinct from the body and other coverings. In the second he realizes the world outside as his own self without losing his identity.

**There are momentary *samādhis* experienced by man in everyday life. In the absence of knowledge they are of no avail to a common man, but to a *yogī* they serve as stepping stones in their endeavour to dive into the depths of their own being.

***It matters not if one is not able to concentrate on the formless aspect of the Divine by means of *nimīlana samādhi*. One is free to concentrate on any external object that attracts the mind and, thus realize one's identity with the whole world which is nothing but *Śiva* in essence. Compare *Vijñāna Bhairava* verse 116 and *Spanda Kārikā* 2/5.

*Lord, hundreds indeed are the rare souls, who, at Thy inspiration, while following pursuits of ploughmen, do behold Thy form face to face with these very eyes. (21)

Not a thought arises that does not constitute Thy will; all acts—meritorious or otherwise—are always being performed by the Lord Himself. Thus, abiding in Thee, I live unfettered, walking the earth willy nilly with nothing to frustrate the festival of the worship of Thy stainless feet. (22)

**Let deep insight into Thy profound thought *thoroughly* dawn on me in the first instance. Having gained strength thereby, let me become endlessly absorbed in Thy worship. (23)

Even in worldly affairs let all this multitude of objects appear to me as Thy part and parcel without evoking *consideration* by itself. (24)

With mind wavering this way and that as a matter of nature, and while attached to its objects, Oh, let me become an unwavering adept in Thy worship. (25)

At Thy own pleasure, O Lord, have I taken birth as Thy servant. None else has a hand in this. Even then, wherefore do I not behold this Thy comely face at any time ? This is indeed strange. (26)

Those who have intense longing for Thee, behold Thee through every object. Oh, what ineffable means must they have come by and what has yielded them the harvest ! (27)

Lord, let all objects appear to me as real, embodying Thy being. Bereft of Thee, let the unreal mean nothing to me. (28)

What is without substance, let that mean nothing to me; what is something be that something to me. In this manner Thou shalt be found and worshipped by me in all states. (29)

HYMN No. 13

In a nutshell, hear, O Lord, here is the outline of joy and sorrow fallen to my lot : joyousness is this Thy communion, and sorrow, Thy separation. (1)

*This is a case of *mahātmās* who have attained spiritual perfection but have a mission in the world. They behave like common men but are alert within. They are rare souls who guide the destiny of mankind.

**Intellectual knowledge is an essential pre-requisite for self-recognition.

The extremely thin film that impairs my vision of Thee even in communion— sweeping away even that in its entirety, reveal, O Lord, Thy stainless form. (2)

Abiding as I am in Thy imperishable body, embracing the whole universe and embodying the bliss of immortal consciousness, worshipping the Lord without a pause, betide what may—life, death or what not. (3)

I am the Lord, I, the luminous; I am omniscient and graceful am I. Who else in the world is the like of me ?—such a feeling of dignity befits none but Thy devotees. (4)

Therefore, with the consciousness of objects as they are in essence, emanating from the destruction of obscurity of Thy immortal oneness, O Lord of *devas*, make me fit for the worship of Thy feet. (5)

*Where meditation is spontaneously followed by vision and touch of the Supreme Lord, let that festival of worship ever attend on me at Thy own inspiration. (6)

The realization of objects as they are in essence and the supreme festival of Thy worship—interlinked as they are, the twain invariably flower in those endowed with devotion. (7)

While constantly sipping the invigorating wine of Thy worship through the medium of all senses from the brimming goblets of all objects, let me become maddened for all time. (8)

Where not a trace of otherness exists, where self-luminosity reigns supreme—in that abode of Thine, Lord, seat me, Thy worshipper. (9)

Supreme Lord, at Thy own pleasure hast Thou ordained me as Thy servant. Wherefore then am I not made worthy of Thy sight or that of shampooing Thy feet ? (10)

**Lord, while showering grace, it is but meet to discriminate; this Thou never dost. What has befallen me now that Thou delayeth revealing Thyself ? (11)

Shining in all objects, external as well as internal, with Thy consort, Oh, would I witness Thee ever worshipped with my own hands as the reality embracing all the three worlds. (12)

*Vide note on verse 9/1.

**The Lord is absolutely free and His will is unfettered. No conditions are attached to His grace. It is difficult for man to understand why and when of it.

Having by the mere will ascended the Lord's mansion without obstruction, let me remain full of bliss with the sport of drinking the highly immortal vintage of Thy grace. (13)

The principle that imparts to all objects of fascinating significance the property of yielding pleasure at the mere touch—those endowed with unflinching devotion worship Thy being by contemplation on that itself. (14)

Being self-luminous Thou illumineth everything; delighting in Thyself, Thou filleth the universe with sweetness. Bubbling with Thy own bliss, the whole world becomes all joy. (15)

*Lord, overcoming delusion, he who beholds all this objective world as Thyself, to that blessed soul, having filled the universe with his own self, whence the fear ? (16)

Lurking in a corner of Thy throat, even the deadly poison, O Lord, is supreme nectar to me, while nectar itself available to me as distinct from Thy being is not to my liking. (17)

Oh, would I have my coutenance ever glowing with strains of love while in communion with Thee; Likewise, let me have my bosom possessed by the sweetheart of Thy worship. (18)

**Ah, the ways of the Supreme Lord admit of no recounting; having given me His own self brimming over with immortality, He does not concede my partaking of it at will. (19)

Entering into Thee, my own being, the fathomless, the undifferentiated, the one, devouring all objectivity, O Lord of *Umā*, let me ever worship and sing of Thee. (20)

HYMN No. 14

In the audience of my Master, the source of all that is of value, let me enjoy the immortal bliss of constant utterance of salutations. (1)

*In the first lap of *sādhanā* a *yogī* strives to realize his own self as distinct from the body and the mind. Thereafter, he realizes the whole world as his own manifestation. This is a state from which there is no apprehension of a fall, and, as such, no fear.

**The author seems to have already experienced the bliss of *samāveśa* at the time of composing this hymn, but was still overwhelmed by *vyutthāna*. His endeavour, therefore, was to attain an uninterrupted state of realization and achieve perfect freedom.

Hail to the one *Rudra*, the one *Śiva*, the *Mahādeva*, the *Maheśvara*, the beloved of *Pārvatī*, *Śarva*, the origin of all gods. (2)

Hail to the Lord of the three worlds, having the eye on the forehead as the symbol of Oneness, Supremacy etc. Hail to the bearer on the throat of the mark of *kālakūṭa* poison as a token of having swallowed the distress of the distressed. (3)

Hail to Him, whose hand shines with the sharp trident symbolizing the three powers*. Hail to the one whose adorable feet fulfil a desire the moment it arises. (4)

Hail to the one having transcendental form emitting manifold beauty. Hail to Thee having on Thy head the ashes of Gaṅgā merged in one tuft of hair. (5)

Hail to Thee having moonlight reflected on the ocean of milk as Thy unction. Hail to Thee embellished with ornaments of snakes dazzling with jewels begotten at the touch of Thy body. (6)

Hail, O Worthy Lord, a resting place for one like the undecaying phase of the moon. Hail to the one eternally annointed by Gaṅgā as the overlord of the universe. (7)

Hail to Thee, the mere touch of whose feet has hallowed the whole bovine family. Hail to him who invariably appears in the congregations organized by devotees. (8)

Hail to Thee, who baffles fools with the guise of ascetics assumed at Thy free will. Hail to Him who merits the good fortune of *Gaurī's* embrace. (9)

Hail to Thee rejoicing in the offerings of emotions steeped in the bliss of love. Hail to Thee, propitiated by hymns and dancings of devotees maddened by the intensity of love. (10)

Hail, O origin and end of the glory of *Brahmā* and other gods. Hail to Thee, whose commands are carried out by the hosts of the overlords of the universe. (11)

Hail to Thee, having revealed Thy authority by pressing Thy signet on the whole universe. Hail to Thee, O Supreme Lord, O Lord of the universe into which Thou hast infused life by self-abandonment. (12)

*The three powers are the three *śaktis* of *icchā*, *jñāna* and *kriyā*.

Hail to Thee having no second when the will to create the three worlds arises. Hail to Thee having the only help-mate in the *Devī*, the repository of all Thy potentialities. (13)

*Hail to Thee, who pervades the three worlds without method. Hail to Thee, the utterance of whose name-sound *Īśvara* is not hated even by fools. (14)

Hail to Thee with innate glory not measured by compassion and other qualities; hail to Thee, the unique terror for the destruction of the dreadful great death. (15)

Hail to Thee, with none to obstruct the ghastly act of universal holocaust; hail to Thee, the utterance of whose name is followed by a thousand beneficient qualities. (16)

Hail to Thee, who gave away this ocean, the source of nectar, as a matter of play; hail to Thee, whose momentary fire of wrath is able to cause universal holocaust. (17)

Hail, O one torch for worldly beings, blinded by the darkness of delusion; hail, O Primary Being ever awake amidst the sleeping world. (18)

Hail, O Golden Oriole, singing within the mountain thicket of the body; hail, O Holy Swan, sporting on the skies of the mind-lakes of good men. (19)

Hail, O Lord of the mountain (Meru) formed of the most exalted of metals—gold; hail to Thee, the evil portent for the reprobates on whom descends the meteor of Thy blasphemy. (20)

Hail, O Thou difficult of attainment by *munis* and *devas* tormented with austere penances; hail, O Thou easy of realization by the community of devotees in all states. (21)

Hail to Thee, who has made those who have taken refuge in Thee as worthy of Thy wealth; hail to Thee, whose only purpose is to take care of those who have sought Thy asylum. (22)

Hail to Thee, having creation, preservation and dissolution as the one glorious act; hail, the great joy of *Utpala*, whose activities are rendered delightful by devotion. (23)

Hail, O worthy of devotion; hail, O conqueror of birth, old age and death; hail, O Patriarch of the world, hail, hail, O three-eyed Lord. (24)

*The reference is to *Bhagavān Viṣṇu* who, as the incarnation of *Vāmana* conquered the three worlds one after another, whereas *Śiva* pervades all the three worlds simultaneously.

HYMN NO. 15

*There are scriptures capable of removing the three impurities, and there are those who have mastered them. In good sooth, Thy devotees are the real masters, the *yogīs*, the wise and the self-poised. (1)

**Appeased with the food of *Kāla*, *Niyati*, *Rāga* and others, the products of *Māyā*, the blest devotees stroll on the shores of the world. (2)

Weeping or laughing, they pre-eminently commune with Thee. Having the utterance of hymns as their pastime, they are the real devotees and form a class by themselves. (3)

Neither an ascetic nor a wielder of supernatural powers, nor would I like to be a worshipper craving for salvation. Only would I remain drunk with the celestial wine of intense love. (4)

Having drawn the outside world into his own heart, he who worships Thee, Lord, with streaming nectar of love, to him I bow. (5)

In the midst of righteousness and unrighteousness, amidst action and knowledge, amidst weal and woe, Oh, the lovers experience something unspeakable. (6)

O Master, father of all that moves and stands, even the blind and the leprous look highly graceful when adorned with Thy supreme love. (7)

Lord, those inflamed with Thy love, though pale in body, having gleanings of grains and feathers of birds as food and raiment hold sway over the Lord of wealth himself. (8)

Rolling in Thy love steeped in immortality and abiding in Thee with their whole being, some rare seekers, O Lord, adore thee with just their hearts. (9)

It is worhty of preservation and augmentation and demands great attention, O Lord, this the supreme wealth of Thy devotion, that is capable of removing all the adversities of the world. (10)

*The three impurities are the three *malas*, that is, *āṇava*, *Māyīya* and *kārma*. For further elucidation compare Introduction, pp. 44.

**These are the six *kañcukas* or coverings of *Māyā* as discussed in Introduction, pp. 43-44.

*Even though the community of devotees is enamoured of Thee, O Master, yet giving up all rivalry, let the Mistress be ever pleased with them. (11)

With the birth of Thy devotion union with Thee is inevitable. Having procured a large pitcher of milk, vain is the quest for curds. (12)

**Oh, is it not a *siddhi* par excellence or does it not shower bliss supreme ?—this devotion to *Śambhu,* which led up in a crescendo becomes everlasting. (13)

Alas, the exquisite jewel of Thy love has become lost in my dark mind and does not manifest those innate super-human flashes of its own richness. (14)

Love for Thee, the Lord, master of the three worlds, is verily the supreme *siddhi*; yet in absence of *aṇimā* and others it is not perfect—this is my anguish. (15)

***Blest are the *yogins,* emitting sweet odour of the bunch of *Śiva* flowers, brightly abloom within and without. They lend fragrance even to those living nearby with perverse tendencies. (16)

****Where light exists not even in name, where the whole world remains fast asleep—in that state of *Śiva's* night the devotees adore Thee without a pause. (17)

Let *sattva* shine forth in the worship of *Śiva,* the Lord of True attributes; let piles of dust from the feet of the Lord

*Śakti is the gateway to *Śiva,* and as such it is essential to invoke Her grace for the success of spiritual effort.

**Absence of *siddhis* was a source of anguish to the author not because he wanted to utilize them, but because he wanted to mark the progress in his spiritual endeavour. These powers appear generally as obstacles in the path, and wise *Sādhakas* do not attach much importance to them in the face of devotion to the lotus feet of the Lord.

***When a man is fully established in *yoga* his body begins to exude fragrance among other characteristics. Contact with them is of great help in keeping the mind free from the bad odour of *vāsanās* in the same way as *Śiva* flowers lend fragrance to others in the vicinity. *Śiva* is a white flower (*dhatūrā*) used in the worship of *Śiva.*

****Śivarātri* is the state of *Śiva* consciousness in which a devotee adores the Lord without a break. It is called night because the world of relativity fades into oblivion. It is a self-luminous state in which the external sources of light play no part.

shine as *rajas* on my crown; let *tamas* come into full play to obliterate all traces of attachment and other mnemonic impressions. Lord, let the conglomerate of all my three *guṇas* unite to get merged into Thy being. (18)

Endless is the cycle of birth and death; the slender frame gets withered by diseases sharp and diverse. Sense pleasures I did not enjoy. What little happiness I came by on occasions did not endure. Thus, born in vain, grant, O Lord, that Thy devotee with the head illumined by the touch of the feet of the crescent-bedecked Lord here and now attains sublime and lasting wealth. (19)

HYMN NO. 16

What is not there for the worldling to conceal Thee? To lovers, however, there is nothing to thwart Thy vision. (1)

Attainable by a succession of disciplines and full of attributes as Thou art, to lovers Thy being appeareth at all times in Thy pure form. (2)

*Triumphant, they laugh; vanquished, they still laugh—those chosen few, who, O Lord, are maddened with the immortal drink of Thy love. (3)

Let me abound in sweet and consummate bliss of Thy love and not achieve insipid *siddhi* or even liberation. (4)

Lord, let this zest of devotion, unknown before, reach its climax the same way as it emanated in me. (5)

In sooth, Lord, there is no scope for another entreaty in me; only let me for all time be seized with nothing but ineffable love. (6)

*In the drunkenness of love, let me be enraged with and pitiful for the world. Likewise, let me laugh and weep and chant the word *Śiva* at the top of my voice. (7)

*Under the spell of devotion, O Lord, let me be distressed yet balanced, weeping yet laughing, disinterested yet serious. (8)

*When a devotee reaches an advanced stage of *sādhanā* he generally behaves like a madman. He laughs and weeps for no visible reason and his *sādhanā* is carried on spontaneously without his being aware of it.

Within or without, Thy lovers know of naught where Thou art not directly present as the indeterminate conscious principle. (9)

Though pierced within by sharp needles of hair standing on end, Thy lovers are verily enraptured by drops of nectar, as it were, even on feigning to listen to Thy blasphemy. (10)

However painful a sensation, it becomes the means of enjoyment to lovers whose consciousness is wholly suffused with nectar of the nature of moonlight. (11)

Within or without, living in whatever state, the devotees equally enjoy undiluted bliss of the touch of Thy being. (12)

*Eliminating from Thy worship the plaintive element of devotion presupposing duality, the chosen few enjoy, O Lord, Thy stainless form of immortality. (13)

The knowers of *śāstras* fall into delusion and so remain estranged. Estrangement is verily the outcome of delusion. To lovers, however, Thou shineth as the one essence without a rival. (14)

How can he be like a common man—the lover, whose mind has become pure by consuming fame and ignominy, attachment and aversion? (15)

Those who have overcome even the gloom of attachment and aversion by the light of devotion—What position do the followers of the path of knowledge hold before these great souls ? (16)

He whose way of *sādhanā* consists of bathing in and drinking of the nectar of love and the like, for him there is rest in supreme peace in the initial, the middle and the final states. (17)

Thou alone being the burden of their songs, the subject of their musings, the object of quest and worship, praiseworthy is, therefore, Thy lover's pilgrimage of life lived in harmony with Thee. (18)

What goes by the name of liberation is but the ripeness of Thy love. Having set foot on the initial stage of that, we are well-nigh liberated. (19)

With the mind brimming over with Thy love, let even woe betide me; with back turned on Thee, let me not have even an endless chain of happiness. (20)

**Bhakti* no doubt starts with a sense of duality but culminates in total oneness with the object of worship. All plaintiveness ceases automatically.

*Lord, Thou art pleased with devotion; devotion again dawns at Thy pleasure. How this inter-dependence works, Thou alone knoweth. (21)

With form or without form, within or without, to the inebriates of love Thou art, O Lord, the embodiment of immortality in every way. (22)

In this very world there exists for Thy lovers a different world which bears exultation as the fruit. (23)

Devotion to Thee, the mysterious, devotion to Thee, the transcendent, devotion to Thee, the Supreme Lord of the universe. Devotion to thee, the *Śambhu,* to *Śiva,* O *Deva* is something that surpasses imagination. (24)

Devotion, devotion, devotion to the Transcendent. Oh, intense devotion—what makes me cry hoarse is, let me have intense devotion for Thee and Thee alone. (25)

**O Lord, the fountain-head of all beauty as Thou art, at Thy touch everything becomes invaluable—be that a jewel or a piece of straw. (26)

Those who do not part with Thee during the process of sense-perceptions right from the subject to the object exalted are such votaries of Thine. (27)

Master, some embrace Thee outside the society of the world; in the heat of love others embrace Thee in the midst of the world itself giving up all regulations. (28)

I bow to *Śiva,* who during the festival of dissolution is passionately and firmly clasped by his *Śakti,* through whom the entire universe is enjoyed by means of drinking, eating and decoration. (29)

*Devotion and God's grace are inter-dependent. The one is not possible without the other. In fact, they are two faces of the same coin. How they operate is only known to the Lord, and is beyond the understanding of man. Also compare verse 8/1.

**High birth is no qualification for salvation. God's name is the only purifier of the body and the mind. Devotees of God, though of humble birth, are as much adorable as God Himself, while those who are devoid of God's love are to be shunned as impure.

*Exalted is Thy unique sovereignty, O Lord of the universe, as there is none to be ruled ever. Likewise, is Thy other state, in which the world appeareth not as it doth now. (30)

HYMN NO. 17

Oh, exalted is this supreme festival of worship—ineffable and sweet—as an outcome of which even tears yield boundless joy of immortality? (1)

All acts connected with Thy worship are conducive to *siddhi*; to lovers, however, all these are *siddhis* by themselves, being one with Thee. (2)

Those who without a pause ever worship Thee in everything as having simultaneously assumed all forms are verily my chosen deities. (3)

Attaining the joy of Thy touch without meditative effort, is the real act of worship known to lovers. May that ever betide me. (4)

Lovers have always the festival of equinox symbolizing harmony. Their worship always consists of the immortal bliss of love. (5)

**Which knows no beginning and no end and is not limited by time—that act, O Lord, constitutes worship. Thy lovers alone are performers of that. (6)

They are the overlords even of *Brahmā* and the like, they are the receptacles of blessedness—those in whom the festival of worship stays constant in dreamland as in deep sleep. (7)

To lovers the light of worship endures not only during *japa*, oblations, bathing and meditation, but in all states. (8)

From amongst *Brahmā* and others, even from amongst *Brahmarṣis*, who is equal to the happy soul ever enjoying the nectar of Thy worship? (9)

In the supreme festival of Thy worship, the only annihilator of

*The other state next to that of *Śiva* is that of *Sadāśiva*.

**The highest experience is one that is spontaneous, a natural state of one's being. It is a state of permanent *samādhi* brought about by relentless effort. As such it knows no beginning and no end.

the world, whatever attainable, is attained, only the lovers know that. (10)

Rooted in Thy light of consciousness, oh, would I ever worship Thee, Lord, with the movements of the body, the speech and the mind, the products of thirtysix categories. (11)

Happy, enjoying the ecstasy of Thy worship, let all my time become endless. This much I pray. (12)

Lord, let my yearning for enjoying the immortal bliss of Thy worship rise in crescendo day by day, ever yielding rich harvest. (13)

In Thy ocean, brimming over with the one immortal bliss thrown up by the dissolution of the world, oh, would I remain constantly worshipping Thee, the Supreme Self. (14)

Having become guileless by cutting through all the knots of latent desires, the mind-stuff is dedicated by lovers once for all to the sweet act of Thy worship. (15)

The faculties of these senses, while resting on their very objects, provide Thy lovers with the wine of immortality for Thy worship. (16)

To lovers irresistibly inflamed with the blazing heat of intense love, what other means of salvation are needed than diving into the nectar of Thy worship. (17)

Lord, let me have the perpetual joy of drinking the nectar of the worship of Thy feet, the only means of receiving Thy grace.(18)

In all actions and at all times, let me experience, O Lord, the supreme bliss of getting intoxicated with the immortal drink of Thy worship. (19)

The significance of the supreme endeavour of Thy worship is verily obvious to the devotees. They forthwith experience a joy which is beyond expectation. (20)

Methinks, not an iota of the wealth of happiness is experienced by man until the supreme bliss of imbibing the nectar of Thy worship is attained. (21)

During the hours of worship lovers find themselves in coalescence with Thy being with no effort and without having to bother about any accessories. (22)

Nothing remains to be achieved by lovers nor is anything difficult of attainment to them. They walk the earth with no purpose, drunk only with the rapture of Thy worship. (23)

Those who have their consciousness expanded with the exuberance of love, O giver of boons, praiseworthy is their unique mode of worship, untarnished by supplication. (24)

What beauty, what bliss, what other prosperity or what other liberation is not there, where the great transcendent Lord is worshipped? (25)

*Nourished by the supreme nectar of pure love undulating within, let this body of mine become fit for Thy worship. (26)

Though uniquely unfettered in movements, O Lord of the worlds, I would fain become fettered for ever for enjoying the worship of Thy feet. (27)

To the chosen few, who, in the hour of meditation, thirst for Thy vision and touch, well up, O Lord, the soothing, sweet and sprawling lake of Thy worship. (28)

Just as Thou art the only object of the bliss of worship in this world, so also is the lover, O Lord, a fit object for the joy of worship. (29)

Lord, how exalted is this ineffable, sublime festival of Thy worship which reduces even the thirtysix categories to ashes. (30)

Adoration, O Lord, to those by whose water of immortal love even the material of Thy worship becomes worshipful. (31)

At the start of worship, having contemplated on Thee by means of a *mantra*, O Lord, the rare lovers out of ecstasy are not contained in their own transcendent being. (32)

Full of exultation as if having gained kingship, some uncommon lovers in the festival of worship deal out the wine of immortality throughout the world. (33)

Are they gods or liberated souls or what else—those chosen few whose enjoyments consist of constant drinking of the nectar of worship? (34)

Having assimilated the universe in themselves as the material for worship, Oh, the lovers gain ineffable weight and also lightness. (35)

*The body of a *sādhaka* must invariably be pure and strong enough to bear the shock of higher consciousness. A weak body is a liability in the spiritual field. A weak body is not likely to withstand the impact of *samādhi*, and may collapse in the process. The worship alluded to is super-conscious experience and not conventional worship.

To lovers the distraction caused by the projection of senses given to worship, is verily the source of immortality exactly as the disturbance of the ocean of milk was to gods. (36)

Some regard worship as the cow of heaven fulfilling all desires; others, contemplating on the inner being, drink of its sweetness as greater than streams of nectar. (37)

Even the projection of senses known as this world, initiates the lovers into the ineffable supreme festival of worship. (38)

In the fervour of intense love, O Lord, Thy worship as one's own self by no means leads to plaintiveness, but is curiously the supreme fruit of plaintiveness. (39)

Some regard worship as the means of attaining Thy state. To lovers on the other hand, it is the culmination of the joy of attainment of union with Thy being. (40)

Worship, though unconventional in form, undertaken by the unfettered, maddened with love, meets inconceivable end in Thy attainment. (41)

Thou alone, O *Śambhu*, art the true fascinating object of worship that emanates from hearts held spell-bound by experience of the sweet bliss of love. (42)

Lord, let my senses grow full, pure, loving and firm for the act of Thy worship. (43)

*Lord, in the act of Thy worship, the veritable treasure of all worships, Oh, what an ineffable beauty emanates from the group of the senses. (44)

This sort of meekness is only discernible in Thee, O Master, that though the lord of the universe, Thou art worshipped by servants and also attained. (45)

Let the great festival of Thy worship ever emanate to me, the blest, out of the concrete or the abstract, out of existence or non-existence. (46)

*Worship here as elsewhere in the book implies the experience of higher consciousness whose impact on the body is tremendous especially in the initial stages. The body must, therefore, be pure and strong enough to withstand the shoek of the beatific vision. The author was not satisfied with partial experience of the Supreme Being in the introvert state. His aim was to divinize the whole physical organism so as to be able to behold the Lord with these very eyes and worship even blades of grass as *Śiva*. For this integral experience the senses must be pure, strong and full of devotion.

Adoration to those, who, having consecrated to Thee all their desires, anger and vanity, are ever given to Thy worship. With them Thou art really pleased. (47)

Exalted is this, the sublime worship of lovers, which though performed with pieces of straw, is really accomplished with jewels. (48)

HYMN NO. 18

Thy lovers alone, O Lord of the universe, having discovered Thee from within the universe, again find the universe as within Thee since nothing in the world is beyond their reach. (1)

*Thou dominateth one state, another is dominated by Thy consort, containing within her bosom the whole order of material creation. In the final analysis, there is no difference betwixt Thy consort, Thyself and the triune world. (2)

People given to vanity do not cognize the essential nature of objects, though full of beauty on proper investigation. Alas, doomed am I, since the mind, though eager, does not realize here even the very nature of the self ! (3)

Having found rest in his own self, which is of Thy essence, and with the infinite wealth thus obtained, he who worships Thy feet, ever heedless of food and raiment, to him I bow. (4)

This world, though comfortably nestled within Thy body, is smouldering within. At Thy own pleasure grant that here and now I may become imbued with the bliss of adoring Thee. (5)

With mind intent on drinking the nectar of spontaneous worship of Thy pair of lotus feet, let me remain a pilgrim of the world hitting upon nothing but bliss in the entire mass of things. (6)

With Thee clearly shining in all worldly transactions, O Lord, let all things constantly appear to me as coming and going. (7)

Let me for all time move about in Thy realm only or as one with Thee. Let there be not a moment when I do not excel as Thyself. (8)

Śiva and *Śakti* are two aspects of the same reality. *Sādhanā* is the domain of *Śakti* and liberation that of *Śiva*.

Thy lovers, possessing the wealth of Thy worship, sport in this ocean of the world, brimming over with streams of soothing nectar flowing from Thy body. (9)

Lord, in Thy sylvan retreat within my own self, Oh, would I, Thy worshipper, for ever dwell underneath the cool shade of the tree of I-consciousness ! (10)

Lord, do appear before me embellished with three eyes and a trident just as Thou art visible to all beings as light in all things. (11)

Having dedicated to Thee my ego as an offering with devotion based on myness, when shalt Thou be pleased to become everywhere the object of my sight? (12)

*Dwelling in the ocean of supreme immortality with mind absorbed in the mere act of Thy worship, let me undertake all mundane operations, all the same imbibing something ineffable. (13)

All this world is Thy glory. Who on earth is capable of explaining its essence? Leaving aside all this, even Thy wondrous name, form and movements captivate the heart, Hara as Thou art. (14)

**To the inebriates of love there is, O Lord, not the least craving for happiness as a means of overcoming pain. In the audience of the Heart Captivator even the supplication for liberation is not remembered. (15)

Wakefulness, dream or deep sleep—whatever the state—to the lover, with mind tuned to Thee, all this is a great festival. (16)

The modifications of the senses right upto the mind, wholly fickle as they are—how do they, Lord, become firm and steady in knowledge on attaining Thee in the case of those glowing with the wealth of love? (17)

Nothing didst Thou create as distinct from Thyself, nor didst Thou make anything other than bliss. Yet, everything is sore and in disharmony. Obeisance to Thee, O source of unique bewilderment. (18)

*Worldly life is not incompatible with the life of the spirit. One can perform worldly acts without losing one's identity.

**Devotion to the Lord is its own reward and not means to an ead. It is not motivated. All desires melt away when one stands face to face with the Lord enjoying His divine presence.

The impurity of differentiation having been washed away by undulating nectar filling the yawning gap of obscuration, the invincible enemy of doubt having been trampled, let me have Thy vision without interruption. (19)

*Lord, do patently inspire me that I may be seized of Thee for all time, and having come extremely close, earnestly worship Thy real form. (20)

None has the power to praise Thee; nay, verily one has, exquisitely lovely as Thou art. On my part, I always pray of Thee that I may behold the Lord without a pause. (21)

HYMN No. 19

Exalted is *Śiva*, the real tree of heaven, of unique behaviour, the giver of amazing fruit, beyond the scope of prayer. (1)

Everything in the world is without doubt traceable to Thee, my own self, the one source of the multitude of objects. Nonetheless, to me Thou dost not reveal Thy being as my own self leaving alone other things. (2)

The great Lord, the conscious being, possessing the powers of knowledge and action, is verily the reality behind everything; otherwise, even the name would not be possible, not to speak of other things. (3)

Setting me on the path of Thy realization, that filches away terrible suffering, O Master, let me as a consequence attain oneness with Thee. (4)

**When shall *siddhi* bejewelled with remembrance of Thy stainless feet come to me from Thee causing amazement in the hearts of perfected beings? (5)

Lord, when shall I come to behold Thy stainless and exquisite visage discharging torrents of unique nectar drowning the universe in its entirety? (6)

*Devotion is not something to be cultivated at will. It must be God-inspired. Without such an inspiration there can be no devotion nor any progress in the spiritual field.

**The *siddhi* referred to in the verse is the climax of spiritual effort and not the achievement of psychic powers which deflect average seekers from the right path.

Lord, when shall Thy form, appearing for the mere recollection, for ever fill in with streams of sublime nectar the deep fissures obscuring harmony with Thee, which is otherwise known as liberation? (7)

Lord, my mind given to the experience of Thy sublime bliss, does not still become divested of unsteadiness; when shall it? Oh, may it become soon, (8)

Let all pairs of opposites come to me, not as dry and insipid but as dedicated to Thee. (9)

Lord, let Thy stainless rays come face to face before me till the darkness of physical and mental afflictions is totally dispelled. (10)

Grant, O Lord, that the enemies in Thy path that conceal the Ultimate Reality, the thieves of the *guṇas* are subdued by me. (11)

Lord, do fill the lake of my mind with torrents of the nectar of Thy devotion so that these vain desires jump up and take to wings. (12)

Wherefore may not Thy love shine in the state of liberation to one still possessed of mortal characteristics? Therefore, raise, me, O Unborn, to a state of perfection conforming to my state of devotion. (13)

*Hold me not lightly, O Lord, as one carried away by the achievement of scant *siddhis*; in the face of Thy love liberation itself following radiant *siddhis* is of little consequence. (14)

Let the Lord be pleased with the servant of me, this much I pray. A fruit, the giver of which is the Lord of the three worlds Himself cannot become a subject of imagination for the like of us. (15)

In the *mānasa* lake of my mind, brimming over with the immortal joy of remembrance of Thy form, may the lotuses of Thy feet remain ever abloom emitting sublime nectar. (16)

*Here the author admits having achieved *siddhis* against some earlier verses expressing concern over their absence. It is evident that he does not attach much importance to them, and holds them as insignificant in the face of God's love.

This, the Lord, Master of the three *śaktis* is my father and *Bhavānī* is my mother. To me there is no second in the world. With this realization, Oh, would I wander in the height of ecstasy. (17)

HYMN No. 20

I bow to the Master, The Lord of the three worlds, white with ashes, three-eyed, bearing the trident, wearing serpent as the holy thread and bearing the crescent on the forehead. (1)

I bow to the one wearing for white vestures the halo of beams radiating from His own body and the lustrous garland of skulls as ornament for the festival of dance. (2)

I bow to the eternal abodes of blessedness, whose deity is *Hara*, whose behaviour is worthy of *Hara* and whose life force is dedicated to none but Hara. (3)

Over and above Thy overlordship there is yet another sport of Thine, that is, I find spontaneous access to Thy wondrous acts brought about by the mere will. (4)

With all this creation as a mere play-thing in this world honoured light of Thine, how infinite, O Lord, must be Thy bliss? (5)

Wherefore may he not be lovely, who is the beloved *Hara* of *Gaurī*, and also wherefore may not *Hara* (Captivator of Hearts) be the supreme beloved of *Gaurī*? (6)

*Whose root lies in immortal and everlasting contemplation, of that enigmatic blessed tree the branches of sense perception are formed accordingly. (7)

When love-itch rises in crescendo, O Supreme Lord, communion inevitably comes into being as a great pillar of rubbing stone. (8)

*The blessed tree alluded to is the man of realization who draws the power from meditation as does a tree from its roots. A blessed tree of this kind is not swept away by sense perceptions, but continues to maintain its poise with senses wide open.

Adoration to the Master having as pastime the act of creation, delighting in preservation and even satisfied with the food of the triune world. (9)

*Adoration to the blessed souls, who, going nowhere and renouncing nothing, yet behold all this as Thy blest light. (10)

What else is there left to be desired by those rolling in the wealth of love? Poor of it, what else is worthy of being desired? (11)

Where miseries become pleasure; where poison turns into nectar; where the world itself is transmuted into liberation—that is the cult of *Śaṅkara*. (12)

In the start, the middle or the end, there is no pain for those devoted to Thee. Even then, say Lord, wherefore are we afflicted? (13)

To some, O Lord, Thy realization is hitched to knowledge, *yoga* and other disciplines. It is only given to the free-willed devotees that Thou art ever visible. (14)

There is no plaintiveness for devotees nor is there any craving since Thou art identical with their own self. Even then the indefinable word 'O *Śiva*' rings in their mouths in the extrovert state. (15)

The light of all lights, full of Universal I-consciousness as 'all this I am'—that *Kriyā Śakti* of Thine, O Lord, I praise. (16).

All beings including *Brahmā, Indra* and *Viṣṇu* are busy feeding on their objects. Therefore, O *Deva*, I adore the whole universe as Thyself. (17)

On account of the relativity of being and non-being everything apart from me is unreal—this alone, O Lord, is signified by Thy sport of dissolution. (18)

**Śaivism* does not believe in the institution of *sannyāsa*. One can attain self-realization while actively engaged in worldly life.

By the mere recollecting, O Giver of boons, Thy form, though inconceivable, emerges before those who roll in the wealth of love. Likewise, they overcome all causes of anguish. (19)

All vital organs vibrating with delight, being saturated with the wine of Thy love, the daring adventurers dance at night in the company of the hosts of realized souls. (20)

The way in which I started Thy hymns, O *Śambhu*, let all my time endlessly grow firm the same way. (21)

ŚIVASTOTRĀVALĪ OF UTPALADEVA
Sanskrit Text

STOTRA NO. 1

(1)

न ध्यायतो न जपतः स्याद्यस्याविधिपूर्वकम् ।
एवमेव शिवाभासस्तं नुमो भक्तिशालिनम् ॥

(2)

आत्मा मम भवद्भक्तिसुधापानयुवाऽपि सन् ।
लोकयात्रारजोरागात्पलितैरिव धूसरः ॥

(3)

लब्धत्वत्सम्पदां भक्तिमतां त्वत्पुरवासिनाम् ।
सञ्चारो लोकमार्गेऽपि स्यात्तयैव विजृम्भया ॥

(4)

साक्षाद्भवन्मये नाथ सर्वस्मिन् भुवनान्तरे ।
किं न भक्तिमतां क्षेत्रं मन्त्रः क्वैषां न सिध्यति ॥

(5)

जयन्ति भक्तिपीयूषरसासववरोन्मदाः ।
अद्वितीया अपि सदा त्वद्द्वितीया अपि प्रभो ॥

(6)

अनन्तानन्दसिन्धोस्ते नाथ तत्त्वं विदन्ति ते ।
तादृशा एव ये सान्द्रभक्त्यानन्दरसाप्लुताः ॥

(7)

त्वमेवात्मेश सर्वस्य सर्वश्चात्मनि रागवान् ।
इति स्वभावसिद्धां त्वद्भक्तिं जानञ्जयेज्जनः ॥

(8)

नाथ वेद्यक्षये केन न दृश्योऽस्येककः स्थितः ।
वद्यवेदकसंक्षोभेऽप्यसि भक्तैः सुदर्शनः ॥

(9)

अनन्तानन्दसरसी देवी प्रियतमा यथा ।
अवियुक्तास्ति ते तद्वदेका त्वद्भक्तिरस्तु मे ॥

(10)

सर्व एव भवल्लाभहेतुर्भक्तिमतां विभो ।
संविन्मार्गोऽयमाह्लाददुःखमोहैस्त्रिधा स्थितः ॥

(11)

भवद्भक्त्यमृतास्वादाद्बोधस्य स्यात्परापि या ।
दशा सा मां प्रति स्वामिन्नासवस्येव शुक्तता ॥

(12)

भवद्भक्तिमहाविद्या येषामभ्यासमागता ।
विद्याविद्योभयस्यापि त एते तत्त्ववेदिनः ॥

(13)

आमूलाद्वाग्लता सेयं क्रमविस्फारशालिनी ।
त्वद्भक्तिसुधया सिक्ता तद्रसाढ्यफलास्तु मे ॥

(14)

शिवो भूत्वा यजेतेति भक्तो भूत्वेति कथ्यते ।
त्वमेव हि वपुः सारं भक्तैरद्वयशोधितम् ॥

(15)

भक्तानां भवदद्वैतसिद्ध्यै का नोपपत्तयः ।
तदसिद्ध्यै निकृष्टानां कानि नावरणानि वा ॥

(16)

कदाचित्क्वापि लभ्योऽसि योगेनेतीश वञ्चना ।
अन्यथा सर्वकक्ष्यासु भासि भक्तिमतां कथम् ॥

(17)

प्रत्याहाराद्यसंस्पृष्टो विशेषोऽस्ति महानयम् ।
योगिभ्यो भक्तिभाजां यद् व्युत्थानेऽपि समाहिताः ॥

(18)

न योगो न तपो नार्चाक्रमः कोऽपि प्रणीयते ।
अमाये शिवमार्गेऽस्मिन् भक्तिरेका प्रशस्यते ॥

(19)

सर्वतो विलसद्भक्तितेजोध्वस्तावृतेर्मम ।
प्रत्यक्षसर्वभावस्य चिन्तानामापि नश्यतु ॥

(20)

शिव इत्येकशब्दस्य जिह्वाग्रे तिष्ठतः सदा ।
समस्तविषयास्वादो भक्तेष्वेवास्ति कोऽप्यहो ॥

(21)

शान्तकल्लोलशीतास्वच्छस्वादुभक्तिसुधाम्बुधौ ।
अलौकिकरसास्वादे सुस्थैः को नाम गण्यते ॥

(22)

मादृशैः किं न चर्व्यंत भवद्भक्तिमहौषधिः ।
तादृशी भगवन्यस्या मोक्षाख्योऽनन्तरो रसः ॥

(23)

ता एव परमर्थ्यन्ते सम्पदः सद्भिरीश याः ।
त्वद्भक्तिरससम्भोगविस्रम्भपरिपोषिकाः ॥

(24)

भवद्भक्तिसुधासारस्तैः किमप्युपलक्षितः ।
ये न रागादिपङ्केऽस्मिँल्लिप्यन्ते पतिता अपि ॥

(25)

अणिमादिषु मोक्षान्तेष्वङ्गेष्वेव फलाभिधा ।
भवद्भक्तेर्विपक्वाया लताया इव केषुचित् ॥

(26)

चित्रं निसर्गतो नाथ दुःखबीजमिदं मनः ।
त्वद्भक्तिरससंसिक्तं निःश्रेयसमहाफलम् ॥

STOTRA NO. 2

(1)

अग्नीषोमरविब्रह्मविष्णुस्थावरजङ्गम-
स्वरूपबहुरूपाय नमः संविन्मयाय ते ॥

(2)

विश्वेन्धनमहाक्षारानुलेपशुचिवर्चसे ।
महानलाय भवते विश्वैकहविषे नमः ॥

(3)

परमामृतसान्द्राय शीतलाय शिवाग्नये ।
कस्मैचिद्विश्वसंप्लोषविषमाय नमोऽस्तु ते ॥

(4)

महादेवाय रुद्राय शङ्कराय शिवाय ते ।
महेश्वरायापि नमः कस्मैचिन्मन्त्रमूर्तये ॥

(5)

नमो निकृत्तनिःशेषत्रैलोक्यविगलद्वसा-
वसेकविषमायापि मङ्गलाय शिवाग्नये ॥

(6)

समस्तलक्षणायोग एव यस्योपलक्षणम् ।
तस्मै नमोऽस्तु देवाय कस्मैचिदपि शम्भवे ॥

(7)

वेदागमविरुद्धाय वेदागमविधायिने ।
वेदागमसतत्त्वाय गुह्याय स्वामिने नमः ॥

(8)

संसारैकनिमित्ताय संसारैकविरोधिने ।
नमः संसाररूपाय निःसंसाराय शम्भवे ॥

(9)

मूलाय मध्यायाग्राय मूलमध्याग्रमूर्तये ।
क्षीणाग्रमध्यमूलाय नमः पूर्णाय शम्भवे ॥

(10)

नमः सुकृतसम्भारविपाकः सुकृवप्यसौ ।
यस्य नामग्रहः तस्मै दुर्लभाय शिवाय ते ॥

(11)

नमश्चराचराकारपरेतनिचयैः सदा ।
क्रीडते तुभ्यमेकस्मै चिन्मयाय कपालिने ॥

(12)

मायाविने विशुद्धाय गुह्याय प्रकटात्मने ।
सूक्ष्माय विश्वरूपाय नमश्चित्राय शम्भवे ॥

(13)

ब्रह्मेन्द्रविष्णुनिर्व्यूढजगत्संहारकेलये ।
आश्चर्यकरणीयाय नमस्ते सर्वशक्तये ॥

(14)

तटेष्वेव परिभ्रान्तैः लब्धास्तास्ता विभूतयः ।
यस्य तस्मै नमस्तुभ्यमगाधहरसिन्धवे ॥

(15)

मायामयजगत्सान्द्रपङ्कमध्याधिवासिने ।
अलेपाय नमः शम्भुशतपत्राय शोभिने ॥

(16)

मङ्गलाय पवित्राय निधये भूषणात्मने ।
प्रियाय परमार्थाय सर्वोत्कृष्टाय ते नमः ॥

(17)

नमः सततबद्धाय नित्यनिर्मुक्तिभागिने ।
बन्धमोक्षविहीनाय कस्मैचिदपि शम्भवे ।।

(18)

उपहासैकसारेऽस्मिन्नेतावति जगत्त्रये ।
तुभ्यमेवाद्वितीयाय नमो नित्यसुखासिने ।।

(19)

दक्षिणाचारसाराय वामाचाराभिलाषिणे ।
सर्वाचाराय शर्वाय निराचाराय ते नमः ।।

(20)

यथा तथापि यः पूज्यो यत्रतत्रापि योऽर्चितः ।
योऽपि वा सोऽपि वा योऽसौ देवस्तस्मै नमोऽस्तु ते ।।

(21)

मुमुक्षुजनसेव्याय सर्वसन्तापहारिणे ।
नमो विततलावण्यवाराय वराय ते ।।

(22)

सदा निरन्तरानन्दरसनिर्भरिताखिल-
त्रिलोकाय नमस्तुभ्यं स्वामिने नित्यपर्वणे ।।

(23)

सुखप्रधानसंवेद्यसम्भोगैर्भजते च यत् ।
त्वामेव तस्मै घोराय शक्तिवृन्दाय ते नमः ।।

(24)

मुनीनामप्यविज्ञेयं भक्तिसम्बन्धचेष्टिताः ।
आलिङ्गन्त्यपि यं तस्मै कस्मैचिद्भवते नमः ।।

(25)

परमामृतकोशाय परमामृतराशये ।
सर्वपारम्यपारम्यप्राप्याय भवते नमः ।।

(26)

महामन्त्रमयं नौमि रूपं ते स्वच्छशीतलम् ।
अपूर्वामोदसुभगं परामृतरसोल्वणम् ।।

(27)

स्वातन्त्र्यामृतपूर्णत्वबैक्यख्यातिमहापटे ।
चित्रं नास्त्येव यत्रेश तन्नौमि तव शासनम् ।।

(28)

सर्वाशङ्काशनिं सर्वालक्ष्मीकालानलं तथा ।
सर्वमङ्गल्यकल्पान्तं मार्गं माहेश्वरं नमः ॥

(29)

जय देव नमो नमोऽस्तु ते सकलं विश्वमिदं तवाश्रितम् ।
जगतां परमेश्वरो भवान् परमेकः शरणागतोऽस्मि ते ॥

STOTRA NO. 3

(1)

सदसत्त्वेन भावानां युक्ता या द्वितयी गतिः ।
तामुल्लङ्घ्य तृतीयस्मै नमश्चित्राय शम्भवे ॥

(2)

आसुरर्षिजनादस्मिन्नस्वतन्त्रे जगत्त्रये ।
स्वतन्त्रास्ते स्वतन्त्रस्य ये तवैवानुजीविनः ॥

(3)

अशेष-विश्वखचित-भवद्वपुरनुस्मृतिः ।
येषां भवरुजामेकं भेषजं ते सुखासिनः ॥

(4)

सितातपत्रं यस्येन्दुः स्वप्रभापरिपूरितः ।
चामरं स्वर्धुनीस्रोतः स एकः परमेश्वरः ॥

(5)

प्रकाशां शीतलामेकां शुद्धां शशिकलामिव ।
दृशं वितर मे नाथ कामप्यमृतवाहिनीम् ॥

(6)

त्वच्चिदानन्दजलधेश्च्युताः संवित्तिविप्रुषः ।
इमाः कथं मे भगवन्नामृतास्वादसुन्दराः ॥

(7)

त्वयि रागरसे नाथ न मग्नं हृदयं प्रभो ।
येषामहृदया एव तेऽवज्ञास्पदमीदृशाः ॥

(8)

प्रभुणा भवता यस्य जातं हृदयमेलनम् ।
प्राभवीणां विभूतीनां परमेकः स भाजनम् ॥

(9)

हर्षाणामथ शोकानां सर्वेषां प्लावकः समम् ।
भवद्ध्यानामृतापूरो निम्नानिम्नभुवामिव ॥

(10)

केव न स्याद्दशा तेषां सुखसम्भारनिर्भरा ।
येषामात्माधिकेनेश न क्वापि विरहस्त्वया ॥

(11)

गर्जामि बत नृत्यामि पूर्णा मम मनोरथाः ।
स्वामी ममैष घटितो यत्त्वमत्यन्तरोचनः ॥

(12)

नान्यद्वेद्यं क्रिया यत्र नान्यो योगो विदा च यत् ।
ज्ञानं स्यात् किन्तु विश्वैकपूर्णा चित्त्वं विजृम्भते ॥

(13)

दुर्जयानामनन्तानां दुःखानां सहसैव ते ।
हस्तात्पलायिता येषां वाचि शश्वच्छिवध्वनिः ॥

(14)

उत्तमः पुरुषोऽन्योऽस्ति युष्मच्छेषविशेषितः ।
त्वं महापुरुषस्त्वेको निःशेषपुरुषाश्रयः ॥

(15)

जयन्ति ते जगद्वन्द्या दासास्ते जगतां विभो ।
संसारार्णव एवैष येषां क्रीडामहासरः ॥

(16)

आसतां तावदन्यानि दैन्यानीह भवज्जुषाम् ।
त्वमेव प्रकटीभूया इत्यनेनैव लज्ज्यते ॥

(17)

मत्परं नास्ति तत्रापि जापकोऽस्मि तवैक्यतः ।
तत्त्वेन जप इत्यक्षमालया दिशसि क्वचित् ॥

(18)

सतोऽवश्यं परमसत्सच्च तस्मात्परं प्रभो ।
त्वं चासतस्सतश्चान्यस्तेनासि सदसन्मयः ॥

(19)

सहस्रसूर्यकिरणाधिकशुद्धप्रकाशवान् ।
अपि त्वं सर्वभुवनव्यापकोऽपि न दृश्यसे ॥

(20)

जडे जगति चिद्रूपः किल वेद्योऽपि वेदकः ।
विभुर्मितेच येनासि तेन सर्वोत्तमो भवान् ॥

(21)

अलमाक्रन्दितैरन्यैरियदेव पुरः प्रभोः ।
तीव्रं विरौमि यन्नाथ मुह्याम्येवं विदन्नपि ॥

STOTRA NO. 4

(1)

चपलमसि यदपि मानस
तत्रापि श्लाघ्यसे यतो भजसे ।
शरणानामपि शरणं
त्रिभुवनगुरुमम्बिकाकान्तम् ॥

(2)

उल्लङ्घ्य विविधदैवत-
सोपानक्रममुपेयशिवचरणान् ।
आश्रित्याप्यधरतरां भूमिं
नाद्यापि चित्रमुज्झामि ॥

(3)

प्रकटय निजमध्वानं
स्थगयतरामखिललोकचरितानि ।
यावद्भवामि भगवं
स्तव सपदि सदोदितो दासः ॥

(4)

शिव शिव शम्भो शङ्कर
शरणागतवत्सलाशु कुरु करुणाम् ।
तव चरणकमलयुगल-
स्मरणपरस्य हि सम्पदोऽदूरे ॥

(5)

तावकाङ्घ्रिकमलासनलीना
ये यथारुचि जगद्रचयन्ति ।

ते विरिञ्चिमधिकारमलेना-
लिप्तमस्ववशमीश हसन्ति ॥

(6)

त्वत्प्रकाशवपुषो न विभिन्नं
किञ्चन प्रभवति प्रतिभातुम् ।
तत्सदैव भगवन् परिलब्धो-
ऽसीश्वर प्रकृतितोऽपि विदूरः ॥

(7)

पादपङ्कजरसं तव केचिद्
भेदपर्युषितवृत्तिमुपेताः ।
केचनापि रसयन्ति तु सद्यो
भातमक्षतवपुर्द्वयशून्यम् ॥

(8)

नाथ विद्युदिव भाति विभाते
या कदाचन ममामृतदिग्धा ।
सा यदि स्थिरतरैव भवेत्तत्
पूजितोऽसि विधिवत्किमुतान्यत् ॥

(9)

सर्वमस्य परमस्ति न किञ्चिद्
वस्त्ववस्तु यदि वेत्ति महत्या ।
प्रज्ञया व्यवसितोऽत्र यथैव
त्वं तथैव भव सुप्रकटो मे ॥

(10)

स्वेच्छयैव भगवन्निजमार्गे
कारितः पदमहं प्रभुणैव ।
तत्कथं जनवदेव चरामि
त्वत्पदोचितमवैमि न किञ्चित् ॥

(11)

कोऽपि देव हृदि तेषु तावको
जृम्भते सुभगभाव उत्तमः ।
त्वत्कथाम्बुदनिनादचातका
येन तेऽपि सुभगीकृताश्चिरम् ॥

(12)

त्वज्जुषां त्वयि कयापि लीलया
राग एष परिपोषमागतः ।
यद्वियोगभुवि सङ्कथा तथा
संस्मृतिः फलति सङ्गमोत्सवम् ॥

(13/14)

यो विचित्ररससेकवर्धितः
शङ्करेति शतशोऽप्युदीरितः ।
शब्द आविशति तिर्यगाशये-
ष्वप्ययं नवनवप्रयोजनः ॥
ते जयन्ति मुखमण्डले भ्रमन् ।
अस्ति येषु नियतं शिवध्वनिः ।
यः शशीव प्रसृतोऽमृताशयात्
स्वादु संस्रवति चामृतं परम् ॥

(15)

परिसमाप्तमिवोग्रमिदं जगद्
विगलितोऽविरलो मनसो मलः ।
तदपि नास्ति भवत्पुरगोपुरा-
र्गलकवाटविघट्टनमण्वपि ॥

(16)

सततफुल्लभवन्मुखपङ्कजो-
दरविलोकनलालसचेतसः ॥
किमपि तत्कुरु नाथ मनागिव
स्फुरसि येन ममाभिमुखस्थितिः ॥

(17)

त्वदविभेदमतेरपरं नु किं
सुखमिहास्ति विभूतिरथापरा ।
तदिह तावकदासजनस्य किं
कुपथमेति मनः परिहृत्य ताम् ॥

(18)

क्षणमपीह न तावकदासतां
प्रति भवेयमहं किल भाजनम् ।

भवदभेदरसासवमादरा-
दविरतं रसयेयमहं न चेत् ॥

(19)

न किल पश्यति सत्यमयं जन-
स्तव वपुर्द्वयदृष्टिमलीमसः ।
तदपि सर्वविदाश्रितवत्सलः
किमिदमारटितं न शृणोषि मे ॥

(20)

स्मरसि नाथ कदाचिदपीहितं
विषयसौख्यमथापि मयार्थितम् ।
सततमेव भवद्वपुरीक्षणा-
मृतमभीष्टमलं मम देहि तत् ॥

(21)

किल यदैव शिवाध्वनि तावके
कृतपदोऽस्मि महेश तवेच्छया ।
शुभशतान्युदितानि तदैव मे
किमपरं मृगये भवतः प्रभो ॥

(22)

यत्र सोऽस्तमयमेति विवस्वां-
श्चन्द्रमः प्रभृतिभिः सह सर्वैः ।
कापि सा विजयते शिवरात्रिः
स्वप्रभाप्रसरभास्वररूपा ॥

(23)

अप्युपार्जितमहं त्रिषु लोके-
ष्वाधिपत्यममरेश्वर मन्ये ।
नीरसं तदखिलं भवदङ्घ्रि-
स्पर्शनामृतरसेन विहीनम् ॥

(24)

बत नाथ दृढोऽयमात्मबन्धो
भवदख्यातिमयस्त्वयैव क्लृप्तः ।
यदयं प्रथमानमेव मे त्वा-
मवधीर्य श्लथते न लेशतोऽपि ॥

(25)

महताममरेश पूज्यमानो-
ऽप्यनिशं तिष्ठसि पूजकैकरूपः ।
बहिरन्तरपीह दृश्यमानः
स्फुरसि द्रष्टृशरीर एव शश्वत् ॥

STOTRA NO. 5

(1)

त्वत्पादपद्मसम्पर्कमात्रसम्भोगसङ्गिनम् ।
गलेपादिकया नाथ मां स्ववेश्म प्रवेशय ॥

(2)

भवत्पादाम्बुजरजोराजिरञ्जितमूर्धजः ।
अपाररभसारब्धनर्तनः स्यामहं कदा ॥

(3)

त्वदेकनाथो भगवन्नियदेवार्थये सदा ।
त्वदन्तर्वसतिमूको भवेयं मान्यथा बुधः ॥

(4)

अहो सुधानिधे स्वामिन् अहो मृष्ट त्रिलोचन ।
अहो स्वादो विरूपाक्षेत्येव नृत्येयमारटन् ॥

(5)

त्वत्पादपद्मसंस्पर्शपरिमीलितलोचनः ।
विजृम्भेय भवद्भक्तिमदिरामदघूर्णितः ॥

(6)

चित्तभूभृद्भुवि विभो वसेयं क्वापि यत्र सा ।
निरन्तरत्वत्प्रलापमयी वृत्तिर्महारसा ॥

(7)

यत्र देवीसमेतस्त्वमासौधादा च गोपुरात् ।
बहुरूपः स्थितस्तस्मिन्वास्तव्यः स्यामहं पुरे ॥

(8)

समुल्लसन्तु भगवन् भवद्भानुमरीचयः ।
विकसत्वेष यावन्मे हृत्पद्मः पूजनाय ते ॥

(9)

प्रसीद भगवन् येन त्वत्पदे पतितं सदा ।
मनो मे तत्तदास्वाद्य क्षीबेदिव गलेदिव ॥

(10)

प्रहर्षाद्वाथ शोकाद्वा यदि कुड्याद्घटादपि ।
बाह्यादथान्तराद्भावात्प्रकटीभव मे प्रभो ॥

(11)

बहिरप्यन्तरपि तत्स्यन्दमानं सदास्तु मे ।
भवत्पादाम्बुजस्पर्शामृतमत्यन्तशीतलम् ॥

(12)

त्वत्पादसंस्पर्शसुधासरसोऽन्तर्निमज्जनम् ।
कोऽप्येष सर्वसम्भोगलङ्घी भोगोऽस्तु मे सदा ॥

(13)

निवेदितमुपादत्स्व रागादि भगवन्मया ।
आदाय चामृतीकृत्य भुङ्क्ष्व भक्तजनैः समम् ॥

(14)

अशेषभुवनाहारनित्यतृप्तः सुखासनम् ।
स्वामिन् गृहाण दासेषु प्रसादालोकनक्षणम् ।

(15)

अन्तर्भक्तिचमत्कारचर्वणामीलितेक्षणः ।
नमो मह्यं शिवायेति पूजयन् स्यां तृणान्यपि ॥

(16)

अपि लब्धमवद्भावः स्वात्मोल्लासमयं जगत् ।
पश्यन् भक्तिरसाभोगैर्भवेयमवियोजितः ॥

(17)

आकाङ्क्षणीयमपरं येन नाथ न विद्यते ।
तव तेनाद्वितीयस्य युक्तं यत्परिपूर्णता ॥

(18)

हस्यते नृत्यते यत्र रागद्वेषादि भुज्यते ।
पीयते भक्तिपीयूषरसस्तत्प्राप्नुयां पदम् ॥

(19)

तत्तदपूर्वामोदत्वच्चिन्ताकुसुमवासना दृढताम् ।
एतु मम मनसि यावन्नश्यतु दुर्वासनागन्धः ॥

(20)

क्व नु रागादिषु रागः
क्व च हरचरणाम्बुजेषु रागित्वम् ।
इत्थं विरोधरसिकं
बोधय हितममर मे हृदयम् ॥

(21)

विचरन्योगदशास्वपि
विषयव्यावृत्तिवर्तमानोऽपि ।
त्वच्चिन्तामदिरामद-
तरलीकृतहृदय एव स्याम् ॥

(22)

वाचि मनोमतिषु तथा
शरीरचेष्टासु करणरचितासु ।
सर्वत्र सर्वदा मे
पुरःसरो भवतु भक्तिरसः ॥

(23)

शिव-शिव-शिवेति नामनि
तव निरवधि नाथ जप्यमानेऽस्मिन् ।
आस्वादयन् भवेयं
कमपि महारसमपुनरुक्तम् ॥

(24)

स्फुरदनन्तचिदात्मकविष्टपे
परिनिपीतसमस्तजडाध्वनि ।
अगणितापरचिन्मयगण्डिके
प्रविचरेयमहं भवतोऽर्चिता ॥

(25)

स्ववपुषि स्फुटभासिनि शाश्वते
स्थितिकृते न किमप्युपयुज्यते ।
इति मतिः सुदृढा भवतात् परं
मम भवच्चरणाब्जरजः शुचेः ॥

(26)

किमपि नाथ कदाचन चेतसि
स्फुरति तद्भवदङ्घ्रितलस्पृशाम् ।

गलति यत्र समस्तमिदं सुधा-
सरसि विश्वमिदं विश मे सदा ॥

STOTRA NO. 6

(1)

क्षणमात्रमपीशान वियुक्तस्य त्वया मम ।
निबिडं तप्यमानस्य सदा भूया दृशः पदम् ॥

(2)

वियोगसारे संसारे प्रियेण प्रभुणा त्वया ।
अवियुक्तः सदैव स्यां जगतापि वियोजितः ॥

(3)

कायवाङ्मनसैर्यत्र यामि सर्वं त्वमेव तत् ।
इत्येष परमार्थोऽपि परिपूर्णोऽस्तु मे सदा ॥

(4)

निर्विकल्पो महानन्दपूर्णो यद्वद्भवांस्तथा ।
भवत्स्तुतिकरी भूयादनुरूपैव वाङ् मम ॥

(5)

भवदावेशतः पश्यन् भावं भावं भवन्मयम् ।
विचरेयं निराकाङ्क्षः प्रहर्षपरिपूरितः ॥

(6)

भगवन्भवतः पूर्णं पश्येयमखिलं जगत् ।
तावतैवास्मि सन्तुष्टस्ततो न परिखिद्यसे ॥

(7)

विलीयमानास्त्वय्येव व्योम्नि मेघलवा इव ।
भावा विभान्तु मे शश्वत्क्रमनैर्मल्यगामिनः ॥

(8)

स्वप्रभाप्रसरध्वस्तापर्यन्तध्वान्तसन्ततिः ।
सन्ततं भातु मे कोऽपि भवमध्याद्भवन्मणिः ।

(9)

कां भूमिकां नाधिशेषे किं तत्स्याद्यन्न ते वपुः ।
श्रान्तस्तेनाप्रयासेन सर्वतस्त्वामवाप्नुयाम् ॥

(10)

भववङ्गपरिष्वङ्गसम्भोगः स्वेच्छयैव मे ।
घटतामियति प्राप्ते किं नाथ न जितं मया ॥

(11)

प्रकटीभव नान्याभिः प्रार्थनाभिः कदर्थनाः ।
कुर्मस्ते नाथ ताम्यन्तस्त्वामेव मृगयामहे ॥

STOTRA NO. 7

(1)

त्वय्यानन्दसरस्वति
समरसतामेत्य नाथ मम चेतः ।
परिहरतु सकृदियन्तं
भेदाधीनं महानर्थम् ॥

(2)

एतन्मम न त्विदमिति
रागद्वेषादिनिगडदृढमूले ।
नाथ भवन्मयतैक्य-
प्रत्ययपरशुः पतत्वन्तः ॥

(3)

गलतु विकल्पकलङ्कावली
समुल्लसतु हृदि निरर्गलता ।
भगवन्नानन्दरसा-
प्लुतास्तु मे चिन्मयी मूर्तिः ।

(4)

रागादिमयभवाण्डक-
लुठितं त्वद्भक्तिभावनाम्बिका तैस्तैः ।
आप्याययतु रसैर्मा
प्रवृद्धपक्षो यथा भवामि खगः ॥

(5)

त्वच्चरणभावनामृत-
रससारास्वादनैपुणं लभताम् ।

चित्तमिदं निःशेषित-
विषयविषासङ्गवासनावधि मे ।

(6)

त्वद्भक्तितपनदीधिति-
संस्पर्शवशान्ममैष दूरतरम् ।
चेतोमणिर्विमुञ्चतु
रागादिक-तप्तवह्निकणान् ॥

(7)

तस्मिन्पदे भवन्तं
सततमुपश्लोकयेयमत्युच्चैः ।
हरिहयशर्वविरिञ्चा
अपि यत्र बहिः प्रतीक्षन्ते ॥

(8)

भक्तिमदजनितविभ्रम-
वशेन पश्येयमविकलं करणैः ।
शिवमयमखिलं लोकं
क्रियाश्च पूजामयी सकलाः ॥

(9)

मामकमनोगृहीत-
त्वद्भक्तिकुलाङ्गनाणिमाविसुतान् ।
सूत्वा सुबद्धमूला
ममेति बुद्धिं दृढीकुरुताम् ॥

STOTRA NO. 8

(1)

यः प्रसादलव ईश्वरस्थितो
या च भक्तिरिव मामुपेयुषी ।
तौ परस्परसमन्वितौ कदा
तादृशे वपुषि रूढिमेष्यतः ॥

(2)

त्वत्प्रभुत्वपरिचर्वणजन्मा
कोऽप्युदेतु परितोषरसोऽन्तः ।
सर्वकालमिह मे परमस्तु
ज्ञानयोगमहिमादि विदूरे ॥

(3)

लोकवद्भवतु मे विषयेषु
स्फीत एव भगवन्परितर्षः ।
केवलं तव शरीरतयैतान्
लोकयेयमहमस्तविकल्पः ॥

(4)

देहभूमिषु तथा मनसि त्वं
प्राणवर्त्मनि च भेदमुपेते ।
संविदः पथिषु तेषु च तेन
स्वात्मना मम भव स्फुटरूपः ॥

(5)

निजनिजेषु पदेषु पतन्त्विमा
करणवृत्तय उल्लसिता मम ।
क्षणमपीश मनागपि मैव भूत्
त्वदविभेदरसक्षतिसाहसम् ॥

(6)

लघुमसृणसिताच्छशीतलं
भवदावेशवशेन भावयन् ।
वपुरखिलपदार्थपद्धते-
र्व्यवहाराननतिवर्तयेय तान् ॥

(7)

विकसतु स्ववपुर्भवदात्मकं
समुपयान्तु जगन्ति ममाङ्गताम् ।
व्रजतु सर्वमिदं द्वयवल्गितं
स्मृतिपथोपगमेऽप्यनुपाख्यताम् ॥

(8)

समुदियादपि तादृशतावका-
ननविलोकपरामृतसम्प्लवः ।

मम घटेत यथा भवदद्वया
प्रथनघोरदरीपरिपूरणम् ॥

(9)

अपि कदाचन तावकसङ्गमा-
मृतकणाच्छुरणेन तनीयसा ॥
सकललोकसुखेषु पराङ्मुखो
न भवितास्म्युभयच्युत एव किम् ।

(10)

सततमेव भवच्चरणाम्बुजा-
करचरस्य हि हंसवरस्य मे ।
उपरि मूलतलादपि चान्तरा-
दुपनमत्वज भक्तिमृणालिका ॥

(11)

उपयान्तु विभो समस्तवस्तून्यपि
चिन्ताविषयं दृशः पदं च ।
मम दर्शनचिन्तनप्रकाशा-
मृतसाराणि परं परिस्फुरन्तु ॥

(12)

परमेश्वर तेषु तेषु कृच्छ्रे-
ष्वपि नामोपनमत्स्वहं भवेयम् ।
न परं गतभीस्त्वदङ्गसङ्गा-
दुपजाताधिकसम्मदोऽपि यावत् ॥

(13)

भवदात्मनि विश्वमुम्भितं यद्
भवतैवापि बहिः प्रकाश्यते तत् ।
इति यद्दृढनिश्चयोपजुष्टं
तदिदानीं स्फुटमेव भासताम् ॥

STOTRA NO. 9

(1)

कदा नवरसार्द्रार्द्र-
सम्भोगास्वादनोत्सुकम् ।

प्रवर्तेत विहायान्यन्
मम त्वत्स्पर्शने मनः ॥

(2)

त्वदेकरक्तस्त्वत्पाद-
पूजामात्रमहाधनः ।
कदा साक्षात्करिष्यामि
भवन्तमयमुत्सुकः ॥

(3)

गाढानुरागवशतो
निरपेक्षीभूतमानसोऽस्मि कदा ।
पटपटिति विघटिताखिल-
महार्गलस्त्वामुपैष्यामि ॥

(4)

स्वसंवित्सारहृदया-
धिष्ठानाः सर्वदेवताः ।
कदा नाथ वशीकुर्यां
भवद्भक्तिप्रभावतः ॥

(5)

कदा मे स्याद्विभो भूरि
भक्त्यानन्दरसोत्सवः ।
यदालोकसुखानन्दी
पृथङ्नामापि लप्स्यते ॥

(6)

ईश्वरमभयमुदारं
पूर्णमकारणमपह्नुतात्मानम् ।
सहसाभिज्ञाय कदा
स्वामिजनं लज्जयिष्यामि ॥

(7)

कदा कामपि तां नाथ
तव वल्लभतामियाम् ।
यया मां प्रति न क्वापि
युक्तं ते स्यात्पलायितुम् ॥

(8)

तत्त्वतोऽशेषजन्तूनां
भवत्पूजामयात्मनाम् ।
दृष्ट्यानुमोदितरसा-
प्लावितः स्यां कदा विभो ॥

(9)

ज्ञानस्य परमा भूमि-
र्योगस्य परमा दशा ।
त्वद्भक्तिर्या विभो कर्हि
पूर्णा मे स्यात्तदर्थिता ॥

(10)

सहसैवासाद्य कदा
गाढमवष्टभ्य हर्षविवशोऽहम् ।
त्वच्चरणवरनिधानं
सर्वस्य प्रकटयिष्यामि ॥

(11)

परितः प्रसरच्छुद्ध-
त्वदालोकमयः कदा ।
स्यां यथेश न किञ्चिन्मे
मायाच्छायाबिलं भवेत् ॥

(12)

आत्मसात्कृतनिःशेष-
मण्डलो निर्व्यपेक्षकः ।
कदा भवेयं भगवं-
स्त्वद्भक्तगणनायकः ॥

(13)

नाथ लोकाभिमानाना-
मपूर्वं त्वं निबन्धनम् ।
महाभिमानः कर्हि स्यां
त्वद्भक्तिरसपूरितः ॥

(14)

अशेषविषयाशून्य-
श्रीसमाश्लेषसुस्थितः ।

शयीयमिव शीताङ्घ्रि-
कुशेशययुगे कदा ॥

(15)

भक्त्यासवसमृद्धाया-
स्त्वत्पूजाभोगसम्पदः ।
कदा पारं गमिष्यामि
भविष्यामि कदा कृतिः ॥

(16)

आनन्दबाष्पपूर-
स्खलितपरिभ्रान्तगद्गदाक्रन्दः ।
हासोल्लासितवदन-
स्त्वत्स्पर्शरसं कदाप्स्यामि ॥

(17)

पशुजनसमानवृत्ता-
मवधूय दशामिमां कदा शम्भो ।
आस्वादयेय तावक-
भक्तोचितमात्मनो रूपम् ॥

(18)

लब्धाणिमादिसिद्धि-
र्विगलितसकलोपतापसन्त्रासः ।
त्वद्भक्तिरसायनपान-
क्रीडानिष्ठः कदासीय ॥

(19)

नाथ कदा स तथाविध
आक्रन्दो मे समुच्चरेद् वाचि ।
यत्समनन्तरमेव
स्फुरति पुरस्तावकी मूर्तिः ॥

(20)

गाढगाढभवदङ्घ्रिसरोजा-
लिङ्गनव्यसनतत्परचेताः ।
वस्त्ववस्त्विदमयत्नत एव
त्वां कदा समवलोकयितास्मि ॥

STOTRA NO. 10

(1)

न सोढव्यमवश्यं ते जगदेकप्रभोरिदम् ।
माहेश्वराश्च लोकानामितरेषां समाश्च यत् ॥

(2)

ये सर्वैवानुरागेण भवत्पादानुगामिनः ।
यत्र तत्र गता भोगांस्ते कांश्चिदुपभुञ्जते ॥

(3)

भर्ता कालान्तको यत्र भवांस्तत्र कुतो रुजः ।
तत्र चेतरभोगाशा का लक्ष्मीर्यत्र तावकी ॥

(4)

क्षणमात्रसुखेनापि विभुर्येनासि लभ्यसे ।
तत्रैव सर्वः कालोऽस्य त्वदानन्देन पूर्यते ॥

(5/6)

आनन्दरसबिन्दुस्ते चन्द्रमा गलितो भुवि ।
सूर्यस्तथा ते प्रसृतः संहारी तेजसः कणः ॥
बलिं यामस्तृतीयाय नेत्रायास्मै तव प्रभो ।
अलौकिकस्य कस्यापि माहात्म्यस्यैकलक्ष्मणे ॥

(7)

तेनैव दृष्टोऽसि भवद्दर्शनाद्योऽतिहृष्यति ।
कथञ्चिद् यस्य वा हर्षः कोऽपि तेन त्वमीक्षितः ॥

(8)

येषां प्रसन्नोऽसि विभो यैर्लब्धं हृदयं तव ।
आकृष्य त्वत्पुरात्तैस्तु बाह्यमाभ्यन्तरीकृतम् ॥

(9)

त्वदृते निखिलं विश्वं समदृग्यातमीक्ष्यताम् ।
ईश्वरः पुनरेतस्य त्वमेको विषमेक्षणः ॥

(10)

आस्तां भवत्प्रभावेण विना सत्तैव नास्ति यत् ।
त्वद्दूषणकथा येषां त्वदृते नोपपद्यते ॥

(11)

बाह्यान्तरान्तरायालीकेवले चेतसि स्थितिः ।
त्वयि चेत्स्यान्मम विभो किमन्यदुपयुज्यते ॥

(12)

अन्ये भ्रमन्ति भगवन्नात्मन्येवातिदुःस्थिताः ।
अन्ये भ्रमन्ति भगवन्नात्मन्येवातिसुस्थिताः ॥

(13)

अपीत्वापि भवद्भक्तिसुधामनवलोक्य च ।
त्वामीश त्वत्समाचारमात्रात्सिध्यन्ति जन्तवः ॥

(14)

भृत्या वयं तव विभो तेन त्रिजगतां यथा ।
बिभर्ष्यात्मानमेवं ते भर्त्तव्या वयमप्यलम् ॥

(15)

परानन्दामृतमये दृष्टेऽपि जगदात्मनि ।
त्वयि स्पर्शरसेऽत्यन्ततरमुत्कण्ठितोऽस्मि ते ॥

(16)

देव दुःखान्यशेषाणि यानि संसारिणामपि ।
धृत्याढ्यभवदीयात्मयुतान्यायान्ति सह्यताम् ।

(17)

सर्वज्ञे सर्वशक्तौ च त्वय्येव सति चिन्मये ।
सर्वथाप्यसतो नाथ युक्तास्य जगतः प्रथा ॥

(18/19)

त्वत्प्राणिताः स्फुरन्तीमे गुणा लोष्टोपमा अपि ।
नृत्यन्ति पवनोद्धूताः कार्पासपिचवो यथा ॥

यदि नाथ गुणेष्वात्माभिमानो न भवेत्ततः ।
केन हीयेत जगतस्त्वदेकात्मतया प्रथा ॥

(20)

वन्द्यास्तेऽपि महीयांसः प्रलयोपगता अपि ।
त्वत्कोपपावकस्पर्शपूता ये परमेश्वर ॥

(21)

महाप्रकाशवपुषि विस्पष्टे भवति स्थिते ।
सर्वतोऽपीश तत्कस्मात्तमसि प्रसराम्यहम् ॥

(22)

प्रविभागो भवानेव स्वरूपममृतं मम ।
तथापि मर्त्यधर्माणामहमेवैकमास्पदम् ॥

(23)

महेश्वरेति यस्यास्ति नामकं वाग्विभूषणम् ।
प्रणामाङ्कश्च शिरसि स एवैकः प्रभावितः ॥

(24)

सदसच्च भवानेव येन तेनाप्रयासतः ।
स्वरसेनैव भगवंस्तथा सिद्धिः कथं न मे ॥

(25)

शिवदासः शिवैकात्मा किं यन्नासादयेत्सुखम् ।
तर्प्योऽस्मि देवमुख्यानामपि येनामृतासवैः ॥

(26)

हृन्नाभ्योरन्तरालस्थः प्राणिनां पित्तविग्रहः ।
ग्रससे त्वं महावह्निः सर्वं स्थावरजङ्गमम् ॥

STOTRA NO. 11

(1)

जगदिदमथ वा सुहृदो
बन्धुजनो वा न भवति मम किमपि ।
त्वं पुनरेतत्सर्वं
यदा तदा कोऽपरो मेऽस्तु ॥

(2)

स्वामिन्महेश्वरस्त्वं
साक्षात्सर्वं जगत्त्वमेवेति ।
वस्त्वेव सिद्धिमेत्विति
याच्ञा तत्रापि याच्ञैव ॥

(3)

त्रिभुवनाधिपतित्वमपीह य-
त्तृणमिव प्रतिभाति भवज्जुषः ।
किमिव तस्य फलं शुभकर्मणो
भवति नाथ भवत्स्मरणादृते ॥

(4)

येन नैव भवतोऽस्ति विभिन्नं
किञ्चनापि जगतां प्रभवश्च ।
त्वद्विजृम्भितमतोऽद्भुतकर्म
स्वप्युदेति न तव स्तुतिबन्धः ॥

(5)

त्वन्मयोऽस्मि भववर्चननिष्ठः
सर्वदाहमिति चाप्यविरामम् ।
भावयन्नपि विभो स्वरसेन
स्वप्नगोऽपि न तथा किमिव स्याम् ॥

(6)

ये मनागपि भवच्चरणाब्जो-
द्भूतसौरभलवेन विमृष्टाः ।
तेषु विस्रमिव भाति समस्तं
भोगजातममरैरपि मृग्यम् ॥

(7)

हृदि ते न तु विद्यतेऽन्यवन्य-
द्वचने कर्मणि चान्यदेव शम्भो ।
परमार्थसतोऽप्यनुग्रहो वा
यदि वा निग्रह एक एव कार्यः ॥

(8)

मूढोऽस्मि दुःखकलितोऽस्मि जरादिदोष-
भीतोऽस्मि शक्तिरहितोऽस्मि तवाश्रितोऽस्मि ।
शम्भो तथा कलय शीघ्रमुपैमि येन
सर्वोत्तमां धुरमपोज्झितदुःखमार्गः ॥

(9)

त्वत्कर्णदेशमधिशय्य महार्घभाव-
माक्रन्दितानि मम तुच्छतराणि यान्ति ।
वंशान्तरालपतितानि जलैकदेश-
खण्डानि मौक्तिकमणित्वमिवोद्वहन्ति ॥

(10)

किमिव न लभ्यते बत न तैरपि नाथ जनैः
क्षणमपि कैतवादपि च ये तव नाम्नि रताः ।

शिशिरमयूखशेखर तथा कुरु येन मम
क्षतमरणोऽणिमादिकमुपैमि यथा विभवम् ॥

(11)

शम्भो शर्व शशाङ्कशेखर शिव त्र्यक्षाक्षमालाधर
श्रीमन्नुग्रकपाललाञ्छन लसद्भीमत्रिशूलायुध ।
कारुण्याम्बुनिधे त्रिलोकरचनाशीलोग्रशक्त्यात्मक
श्रीकण्ठाशु विनाशयाशुभभरानाधत्स्व सिद्धिं पराम् ॥

(12)

तत्किं नाथ भवेन्न यत्र भगवान्निर्मातृतामश्नुते
भावः स्यात्किमु तस्य चेतनवतो नाशास्ति यं शङ्करः ।
इत्थं ते परमेश्वराक्षतमहाशक्तेः सदा संश्रितः
संसारेऽत्र निरन्तराधिविधुरः क्लिश्याम्यहं केवलम् ॥

(13)

यद्यप्यत्र वरप्रदोद्धततमाः पीडाजरामृत्यवः
एते वा क्षणमासतां बहुमतः शब्दादिरेवास्थिरः ।
तत्रापि स्पृहयामि सन्ततसुखाकाङ्क्षी चिरं स्थास्नवे
भोगास्वादयुतत्वदङ्घ्रिकमलध्यानाग्र्यजीवातवे ॥

(14)

हे नाथ प्रणतार्तिनाशनपटो श्रेयोनिधे धूर्जटे
दुःखैकायतनस्य जन्ममरणत्रस्तस्य मे साम्प्रतम् ।
तच्चेष्टस्व यथा मनोज्ञविषयास्वादप्रदा उत्तमाः
जीवन्नेव समश्नुवेऽहमचलाः सिद्धीस्त्वदर्चापरः ॥

(15)

नमो मोहमहाध्वान्त-
ध्वंसनानन्यकर्मणे ।
सर्वप्रकाशातिशय-
प्रकाशायेन्दुलक्ष्मणे ॥

STOTRA NO. 12

(1)

सहकारि न किञ्चिदिष्यते
भवतो न प्रतिबन्धकं दृशि ।

भवतैव हि सर्वमाप्लुतं
कथमद्यापि तथापि नेक्षसे ॥

(2)

अपि भावगणादपीन्द्रिय-
प्रचयादप्यवबोधमध्यतः ।
प्रभवन्तमपि स्वतः सदा
परिपश्येयमपोढविश्वकम् ॥

(3)

कथं ते जायेरन्कथमपि च ते दर्शनपथं
व्रजेयुः केनापि प्रकृतिमहताङ्केन खचिताः ।
तथोत्थायोत्थाय स्थलजलतृणादेरखिलतः
पदार्थाद्यान्दृष्टिस्त्रवदमृतपूरैर्विकिरसि ॥

(4)

साक्षात्कृतभवद्रूपप्रसृतामृततर्पिताः ।
उन्मूलिततृषो मत्ता विचरन्ति यथारुचि ॥

(5)

न तदा न सदा न चैकदे-
त्यपि सा यत्र न कालधीर्भवेत् ।
तदिदं भवदीयदर्शनं
न च नित्यं न च कथ्यतेऽन्यथा ॥

(6)

त्वद्विलोकनसमुत्कचेतसो
योगसिद्धिरियती सदास्तु मे ।
यद्विशेयर्मभिसन्धिमात्रत-
स्त्वत्सुधासदनमर्चनाय ते ॥

(7)

निर्विकल्पभवदीयदर्शन-
प्राप्तिफुल्लमनसां महात्मनाम् ।
उल्लसन्ति विमलानि हेलया
चेष्टितानि च वचांसि च स्फुटम् ॥

(8)

भगवन्भवदीयपादयो-
र्निवसन्नन्तर एव निर्भयः ।

भवभूमिषु तासु तास्वहं
प्रभुमर्चयमनर्गलक्रियः ॥

(9)

भवदङ्घ्रिसरोरुहोदरे
परिलीनो गलितापरैषणः ।
अतिमात्रमधूपयोगतः
परितृप्तो विचरेयमिच्छया ॥

(10)

यस्य दम्भादिव भवत्पूजासङ्कल्प उत्थितः ।
तस्याप्यवश्यमुदितं सन्निधानं तवोचितम् ॥

(11)

भगवन्नितरानपेक्षिणा
नितरामेकरसेन चेतसा ।
सुलभं सकलोपशायिनं
प्रभुमातृप्ति पिबेयमस्मि किम् ॥

(12)

त्वया निराकृतं सर्वं हेयमेतत्तदेव तु ।
त्वन्मयं समुपादेयमित्ययं सारसङ्ग्रहः ॥

(13)

भवतोऽन्तरचारि भावजातं
प्रभुवन्मुख्यतयैव पूजितं तत् ।
भवतो बहिरप्यभावमात्रा
कथमीशान भवेत्समर्च्यते वा ॥

(14)

निःशब्दं निर्विकल्पं च निर्व्याक्षेपमथानिशम् ।
क्षोभेऽप्यध्यक्षमीक्षेयं त्र्यक्ष त्वामेव सर्वतः ॥

(15)

प्रकटय निजधाम देव यस्मि-
स्त्वमसि सदा परमेश्वरीसमेतः ।
प्रभुचरणरजःसमानकक्ष्याः
किमविश्वासपदं भवन्ति भृत्याः ॥

(16)

दर्शनपथमुपयातोऽप्यपसरसि
कुतो ममेश भृत्यस्य ।

क्षणमात्रकमिह न भवसि
कस्य न जन्तोर्वृ शोर्विषयः ॥

(17)

ऐक्यसंविदमृताच्छधारया
सन्ततप्रसृतया कदा विभो ।
प्लावनात् परमभेदमानयं-
स्त्वां निजं च वपुराप्नुयां मुदम् ॥

(18)

अहमित्यमुतोऽवरुद्धलोका-
द्भवदीयात्प्रतिपत्तिसारतो मे ।
अणुमात्रकमेव विश्वनिष्ठं
घटतां येन भवेयमर्चिता ते ॥

(19)

अपरिमितरूपमहं
तं तं भावं प्रतिक्षणं पश्यन् ।
त्वामेव विश्वरूपं
निजनाथं साधु पश्येयम् ॥

(20)

भवदङ्गगतं तमेव कस्मा-
न्न मनः पर्यटतीष्टमर्थमर्थम् ।
प्रकृतिक्षतिरस्ति नो तथास्य
मम चेच्छा परिपूर्यते परैव ॥

(21)

शतशः किल ते तवानुभावा-
द्भगवन्केऽप्यमुनैव चक्षुषा ये ।
अपि हालिकचेष्टया चरन्तः
परिपश्यन्ति भवद्वपुः सदाग्रे ॥

(22)

न सा मतिरुदेति या न भवति त्वदिच्छामयी
सदा शुभमथेतरद्भगवतैवमाचर्यते ।
अतोऽस्मि भवदात्मको भुवि यथा तथा सञ्चरन्
स्थितोऽनिशमबाधितत्वदमलाङ्घ्रिपूजोत्सवः ॥

(23)

भवदीयगभीरभाषितेषु
प्रतिभा सम्यगुदेतु मे पुरोऽतः ।
तदनुष्ठितशक्तिरप्यतस्त-
द्भवदर्चाव्यसनं च निर्विरामम् ॥

(24)

व्यवहारपदेऽपि सर्वदा
प्रतिभात्वर्थकलाप एष माम् ।
भवतोऽवयवो यथा न तु
स्वत एवादरणीयतां गतः ॥

(25)

मनसि स्वरसेन यत्र तत्र
प्रचरत्यप्यहमस्य गोचरेषु ।
प्रसृतोऽप्यविलोल एव युष्म-
त्परिचर्याचतुरः सदा भवेयम् ॥

(26)

भगवन्भवदिच्छयैव दास-
स्तव जातोऽस्मि परस्य नात्र शक्तिः ।
कथमेष तथापि वक्त्रबिम्बं
तव पश्यामि न जातु चित्रमेतत ॥

(27)

समुत्सुकास्त्वां प्रति ये भवन्तं
प्रत्यर्थरूपावदलोकयन्ति ।
तेषामहो किं तदुपस्थितं स्यात्
किं साधनं वा फलितं भवेत्तत् ॥

(28)

भावा भावतया सन्तु
भवद्भावेन मे भव ।
तथा न किञ्चिदप्यस्तु
न किञ्चिद्भवतोऽन्यथा ॥

(29)

यन्न किञ्चिदपि तन्न किञ्चिद-
प्यस्तु किञ्चिदपि किञ्चिदेव मे ।

सर्वथा भवतु तावता भवान्
सर्वतो भवति लब्धपूजितः ॥

STOTRA NO. 13

(1)

सङ्ग्रहेण सुखदुःखलक्षणं
मां प्रति स्थितमिदं शृणु प्रभो ।
सौख्यमेष भवता समागमः
स्वामिना विरह एव दुःखिता ॥

(2)

अन्तरप्यतितरामणीयसी
या त्वदप्रथनकालिकास्ति मे ।
तामपीश परिमृज्य सर्वतः
स्वं स्वरूपममलं प्रकाशय ॥

(3)

तावके वपुषि विश्वनिर्भरे
चित्सुधारसमये निरत्यये ।
तिष्ठतः सततमर्चतः प्रभुं
जीवितं मृतमथान्यवस्तु मे ॥

(4)

ईश्वरोऽहमहमेव रूपवान्
पण्डितोऽस्मि सुभगोऽस्मि कोऽपरः ।
मत्समोऽस्ति जगतीति शोभते
मानिता त्वदनुरागिणः परम् ॥

(5)

देवदेव भवदद्वयामृता-
ख्यातिसंहरणलब्धजन्मना ।
तद्यथास्थितपदार्थसंविदा
मां कुरुष्व चरणार्चनोचितम ॥

(6)

ध्यायते तदनु दृश्यते ततः
स्पृश्यते च परमेश्वरः स्वयम् ।

यत्र पूजनमहोत्सवः स मे
सर्वदास्तु भवतोऽनुभावतः ॥

(7)

यद्यथास्थितपदार्थदर्शनं
युष्मदर्चनमहोत्सवश्च यः ।
युग्ममेतदितरेतराश्रयं
भक्तिशालिषु सदा विजृम्भते ॥

(8)

तत्तदिन्द्रियमुखेन सन्ततं
युष्मदर्चनरसायनासवम् ।
सर्वभावचषकेषु पूरिते-
ष्वापिबन्नपि भवेयमुन्मदः ॥

(9)

अन्यवेद्यमणुमात्रमस्ति न
स्वप्रकाशमखिलं विजृम्भते ।
यत्र नाथ भवतः पुरे स्थितिं
तत्र मे कुरु सदा तवार्चितुः ॥

(10)

दासधाम्नि विनियोजितोऽप्यहं
स्वेच्छयैव परमेश्वर त्वया ।
दर्शनेन न किमस्मि पात्रितः
पादसंवहनकर्मणापि वा ॥

(11)

शक्तिपातसमये विचारणं
प्राप्तमीश न करोषि कर्हिचित् ।
अद्य मां प्रति किमागतं यतः
स्वप्रकाशनविधौ विलम्बसे ॥

(12)

तत्र तत्र विषये बहिर्विभा-
त्यन्तरे च परमेश्वरीयुतम् ।

त्वां जगत्त्रितयनिर्भरं सदा
लोकयेय निजपाणिपूजितम् ॥

(13)

स्वामिसौधमभिसन्धिमात्रतो
निर्विबन्धमधिरुह्य सर्वदा ।
स्यां प्रसादपरमामृतासवा-
पानकेलिपरिलब्धनिर्वृतिः ॥

(14)

यत्समस्तसुभगार्थवस्तुषु
स्पर्शमात्रविधिना चमत्कृतिम् ।
तां समर्पयति तेन ते वपुः
पूजयन्त्यचलभक्तिशालिनः ॥

(15)

स्फारयस्यखिलमात्मना स्फुरन्
विश्वमामृशसि रूपमामृशन् ।
यत्स्वयं निजरसेन घूर्णसे
तत्समुल्लसति भावमण्डलम् ॥

(16)

योऽविकल्पमिदमर्थमण्डलं
पश्यतीश निखिलं भवद्वपुः ।
स्वात्मपक्षपरिपूरिते जग-
त्यस्य नित्यसुखिनः कुतो भयम् ॥

(17)

कण्ठकोणविनिविष्टमीश ते
कालकूटमपि मे महामृतम् ।
अप्युपात्तममृतं भवद्वपु-
र्भेदवृत्ति यदि रोचते न मे ॥

(18)

स्वप्रलापमयरक्तगीतिका-
नित्ययुक्तवदनोपशोभितः ।

स्यामथापि भवदर्चनक्रिया-
प्रेयसीपरिगताशयः सदा ॥

(19)

ईहितं न बत पारमेश्वरं
शक्यते गणयितुं तथा च मे ।
दत्तमप्यमृतनिर्भरं वपुः
स्वं न पातुमनुमन्यते तथा ॥

(20)

त्वामगाधमविकल्पमद्वयं
स्वं स्वरूपमखिलार्थघस्मरम् ।
आविशन्नहमुमेश सर्वदा
पूजयेयमभिसंस्तुवीय च ॥

STOTRA NO. 14

(1)

जयलक्ष्मीनिधानस्य निजस्य स्वामिनः पुरः ।
जयोद्घोषणपीयूषरसमास्वादये क्षणम् ॥

(2)

जयैकरुद्रैकशिव महादेव महेश्वर ।
पार्वतीप्रणयिञ्शर्व सर्वगीर्वाणपूर्वज ॥

(3)

जय त्रैलोक्यनाथैकलाञ्छनालिकलोचन ।
जय पीतार्तलोकार्तिकालकूटाङ्ककन्धर ॥

(4)

जय मूर्तत्रिशक्त्यात्मशितशूलोल्लसत्कर ।
जयेच्छामात्रसिद्धार्थपूजार्हचरणाम्बुज ॥

(5)

जय शोभाशतस्यन्दित्रिलोकोत्तरवपुर्धर ।
जयैकजटिकाक्षीणगङ्गाकृत्यात्तभस्मक ॥

(6)

जय क्षीरोदपर्यस्तज्योत्स्नाच्छायानुलेपन ।
जयेश्वराङ्गसङ्गोत्थरत्नकान्ताहिमण्डन ॥

(7)

जयाक्षयैकशीतांशुकलासदृशसंश्रय ।
जय गङ्गासदारब्धविश्वैश्वर्याभिषेचन ॥

(8)

जयाधराङ्गसंस्पर्शपावनीकृतगोकुल ।
जय भक्तिमदाबद्धगोष्ठीनियतसन्निधे ॥

(9)

जय स्वेच्छातपोवेशविप्रलम्भितवालिश ।
जय गौरीपरिष्वङ्गयोग्यसौभाग्यभाजन ॥

(10)

जय भक्तिरसार्द्रार्द्रभावोपायनलम्पट ।
जय भक्तिमदोद्दामभक्तवाङ्नृत्ततोषित ॥

(11)

जय ब्रह्मादिदेवेशप्रभावप्रभवव्यय ।
जयलोकेश्वरश्रेणीशिरोविधृतशासन ॥

(12)

जय सर्वजगन्न्यस्तस्वमुद्राव्यक्तवैभव ।
जयात्मदानपर्यन्तविश्वेश्वर महेश्वर ॥

(13)

जय त्रैलोक्यसर्गेच्छावसरासद्वितीयक ।
जयैश्वर्यभरोद्वाहदेवीमात्रसहायक ॥

(14)

जयाक्रमसमाक्रान्तसमस्तभुवनत्रय ।
जयाविगीतमाबालगीयमानेश्वरध्वने ॥

(15)

जयानुकम्पादिगुणानपेक्षसहजोन्नते ।
जय भीष्ममहामृत्युघटनापूर्वभैरव ॥

(16)

जय विश्वक्षयोच्चण्डक्रियानिष्परिपन्थिक ।
जय श्रेयःशतगुणानुगनामानुकीर्तन ॥

(17)

जय हेलावितीर्णतवमृताकरसागर ।
जय विश्वक्षयाक्षेपिक्षणकोपाशुशुक्षणे ॥

(18)

जय मोहान्धकारान्धजीवलोकैकदीपक ।
जय प्रसुप्तजगतीजागरूकाधिपूरुष ॥

(19)

जय देहाद्रिकुञ्जान्तर्निकूजज्जीवजीवक ।
जय सन्मानसव्योमविलासिवरसारस ॥

(20)

जय जाम्बूनदोदग्रधातूद्भवगिरीश्वर ।
जय पापिषु निर्घोल्कापातनोत्पातचन्द्रमः ॥

(21)

जय कष्टतपःक्लिष्टमुनिदेववुरासद ।
जय सर्ववशारूढभक्तिमल्लोकलोकित ॥

(22)

जय स्वसम्पत्प्रसरपात्रीकृतनिजाश्रित ।
जय प्रपन्नजनतालालनैकप्रयोजन ॥

(23)

जय सर्गस्थितिध्वंसकारणैकावधानक ।
जय भक्तिमदालोललीलोत्पलमहोत्सव ॥

(24)

जय जयभाजन जय जितजन्म-
जरामरण जय जगज्ज्येष्ठ ।
जय जय जय जय जय जय जय
जय जय जय जय जय जय त्र्यक्ष ॥

STOTRA NO. 15

(1)

त्रिमलक्षालिनो ग्रन्थाः सन्ति तत्पारगास्तथा ।
योगिनः पण्डिताः स्वस्थास्त्वद्भक्ता एव तत्त्वतः ॥

(2)

मायीयकालनियतिरागाद्याहारतर्पिताः ।
चरन्ति सुखिनो नाथ भक्तिमन्तो जगत्तटे ॥

(3)

रुदन्तो वा हसन्तो वा त्वामुच्चैः प्रलपन्त्यमी ।
भक्ताः स्तुतिपदोच्चारोपचाराः पृथगेव ते ॥

(4)

न विरक्तो न चापीशो मोक्षाकाङ्क्षी त्वदर्चकः ।
भवेयमपि तूद्रिक्तभक्त्यासवरसोन्मदः ॥

(5)

बाह्यं हृदय एवान्तरभिहृत्यैव योऽर्चति ।
त्वामीश भक्तिपीयूषरसपूरैर्नमामि तम् ॥

(6)

धर्माधर्मात्मनोरन्तः क्रिययोर्ज्ञानयोस्तथा ।
सुखदुःखात्मनोर्भक्ताः किमप्यास्वादयन्त्यहो ॥

(7)

चराचरपतेः स्वामिन् भ्रप्यन्धा अपि कुष्ठिनः ।
शोभन्ते परमुद्दामभवद्भक्तिविभूषणाः ॥

(8)

शिलोञ्छपिच्छकशिपुविच्छायाङ्गा अपि प्रभो ।
भवद्भक्तिमहोष्माणो राजराजमपीशते ॥

(9)

सुधार्द्रायां भवद्भक्तौ लुठताप्यारुरुक्षुणा ।
चेतसैव विभोऽर्चन्ति केचित्त्वामभितः स्थिताः ॥

(10)

रक्षणीयं वर्धनीयं बहुमान्यमिदं प्रभो ।
संसारदुर्गतिहरं भवद्भक्तिमहाधनम् ॥

(11)

नाथ ते भक्तजनता यद्यपि त्वयि रागिणी ।
तथापीर्ष्यां विहायास्यास्तुष्टास्तु स्वामिनी सदा ॥

(12)

भवद्भावः पुरो भावी प्राप्ते त्वद्भक्तिसम्भवे ।
लब्धे दुग्धमहाकुम्भे हता दधनि गृध्नुता ॥

(13)

किमियं न सिद्धिरतुला
किं वा मुख्यं न सौख्यमास्रवति ।
भक्तिरुपचीयमाना
येयं शम्भोः सदातनी भवति ॥

(14)

मनसि मलिने मदीये
मग्ना त्वद्भक्तिमणिलता कष्टम् ।
न निजानपि तनुते तान्
अपौरुषेयान्स्वसम्पदुल्लासान् ॥

(15)

भक्तिभंगवति भवति
त्रिलोकनाथे ननूत्तमा सिद्धिः ।

किन्त्वणिमादिकविरहात्
सैव न पूर्णेति चिन्ता मे ॥

(16)

बाह्यतोऽन्तरपि चोत्कटोन्मिष-
त्त्र्यम्बकस्तवकसौरभाः शुभाः ।
वासयन्त्यपि विरुद्धवासनान्
योगिनो निकटवासिनोऽखिलान् ॥

(17)

ज्योतिरस्ति कथयापि न किञ्चि-
द्विश्वमप्यतिसुषुप्तमशेषम् ।
यत्र नाथ शिवरात्रिपदेऽस्मिन्
नित्यमर्चयति भक्तजनस्त्वाम ॥

(18)

सत्त्वं सत्यगुणे शिवे भगवति स्फारीभवत्वर्चने
चूडायां विलसन्तु शङ्करपदप्रोद्यद्रजःसञ्चयाः ।
रागादिस्मृतिवासनामपि समुच्छेत्तुं तमो जृम्भतां
शम्भो मे भवतात्त्वदात्मविलये त्रैगुण्यवर्गोऽथवा ॥

(19)

संसाराध्वा सुदूरः खरतरविविधव्याधिदग्धाङ्गयष्टिः
भोगा नैवोपभुक्ता यदपि सुखमभूज्जातु तन्नो चिराय ।
इत्थं व्यर्थोऽस्मि जातः शशिधरचरणाक्रान्तिकान्तोत्तमाङ्ग-
स्त्वद्भक्तश्चेति तन्मे कुरु सपदि सहासम्पदो दीर्घदीर्घाः ॥

STOTRA NO. 16

(1)

न किञ्चिदेव लोकानां भवदावरणं प्रति ।
न किञ्चिदेव भक्तानां भवदावरणं प्रति ॥

(2)

अप्युपायक्रमप्राप्यः सङ्कुलोऽपि विशेषणैः ।
भक्तिभाजां भवानात्मा सकृच्छुद्धोऽवभासते ॥

(3)

जयन्तोऽपि हसन्त्येते जिता अपि हसन्ति च ।
भवद्भक्तिसुधापानमत्ताः केऽप्यहेव ये प्रभो ॥

(4)

शुष्कर्कं मैव सिद्धेय मैव मुच्येय वापि तु ।
स्वादिष्ठपरकाष्ठाप्तत्वद्भक्तिरसनिर्भरः ॥

(5)

यथैवाज्ञातपूर्वोऽयं भवद्भक्तिरसो मम ।
घटितस्तद्वदीशान स एव परिपुष्यतु ॥

(6)

सत्येन भगवन्नान्यः प्रार्थनाप्रसरोऽस्ति मे ।
केवलं स तथा कोऽपि भक्त्यावेशोऽस्तु मे सदा ॥

(7)

भक्तिक्षीवोऽपि कुप्येयं भवायानुशयीय च ।
तथा हसेयं रुद्यां च रटेयं च शिवेत्यलम् ॥

(8)

विषमस्थोऽपि स्वस्थोऽपि रुदन्नपि हसन्नपि ।
गम्भीरोऽपि विचित्तोऽपि भवेयं भक्तितः प्रभो ॥

(9)

भक्तानां नास्ति संवेद्यं त्वदन्तर्यदि वा बहिः ।
चिद्धर्मा यत्र न भवान्निर्विकल्पः स्थितः स्वयम् ॥

(10)

भक्ता निन्दानुकारेऽपि तवामृतकणैरिव ।
हृष्यन्त्येवान्तराविद्धास्तीक्ष्णरोमाञ्चसूचिभिः ॥

(11)

दुःखापि वेदना भक्तिमतां भोगाय कल्पते ।
येषां सुधार्द्रा सर्वैव संवित्स्वच्छचन्द्रिकामयी ॥

(12)

यत्र तत्रोपरुद्धानां भक्तानां बहिरन्तरे ।
निर्व्याजं त्वद्वपुःस्पर्शरसास्वादसुखं समम् ॥

(13)

तवेश भक्तेरर्चायां दैन्यांशं द्वयसंश्रयम् ।
विलुप्यास्वादयन्त्येके वपुरच्छं सुधामयम् ॥

(14)

भ्रान्तास्तीर्थदृशो भिन्ना भ्रान्तेरेव हि भिन्नता ।
निष्प्रतिद्वन्द्वि वस्त्वेकं भक्तानां त्वं तु राजसे ॥

(15)

मानावमानरागादिनिष्पाकविमलं मनः ।
यस्यासौ भक्तिमांल्लोकतुल्यशीलः कथं भवेत् ॥

(16)

रागद्वेषान्धकारोऽपि येषां भक्तित्विषा जितः ।
तेषां महीयसामग्रे कतमे ज्ञानशालिनः ॥

(17)

यस्य भक्तिसुधास्नानपानादिविविधिसाधनम् ।
तस्य प्रारब्धमध्यान्तदशासूच्चैः सुखासिका ॥

(18)

कीर्त्यश्चिन्तापदं मृग्यः पूज्यो येन त्वमेव तत् ।
भवद्भक्तिमतां श्लाघ्या लोकयात्रा भवन्मयी ॥

(19)

मुक्तिसंज्ञा विपक्वाया भक्तेरेव त्वयि प्रभो ।
तस्यामाद्यदशारूढा मुक्तकल्पा वयं ततः ॥

(20)

दुःखागमोऽपि भूयान्मे त्वद्भक्तिभरितात्मनः ।
त्वत्पराची विभो मा भूदपि सौख्यपरम्परा ॥

(21)

त्वं भक्त्या प्रीयसे भक्तिः प्रीते त्वयि च नाथ यत् ।
तदन्योन्याश्रयं युक्तं यथा वेत्थ त्वमेव तत् ॥

(22)

साकारो वा निराकारो वान्तर्वा बहिरेव वा ।
भक्तिमत्तात्मनां नाथ सर्वथासि सुधामयः ॥

(23)

अस्मिन्नेव जगत्यन्तर्भवद्भक्तिमतः प्रति ।
हर्षप्रकाशनफलमन्यदेव जगत्स्थितम् ॥

(24)

गुह्ये भक्तिः परे भक्तिर्भक्तिर्विश्वमहेश्वरे ।
त्वयि शम्भौ शिवे देव भक्तिर्नाम किमप्यहो ॥

(25)

भक्तिर्भक्तिः परे भक्तिर्भक्तिर्नाम समुत्कटा ।
तारं विरौमि यत्तीव्रा भक्तिर्मेऽस्तु परं त्वयि ॥

(26)

यतोऽसि सर्वशोभानां प्रसवावनिरीश तत् ।
त्वयि लग्नमनर्घं स्याद्रत्नं वा यदि वा तृणम् ॥

(27)

ग्रावेदकादा च वेद्याद्येषां संवेदनाध्वनि ।
भवता न वियोगोऽस्ति ते जयन्ति भवज्जुषः ॥

(28)

संसारसदसो बाह्ये कैश्चित्त्वं परिरभ्यसे ।
स्वामिन्परैस्तु तत्रैव ताभ्यिद्भिस्त्यक्तयन्त्रणैः ॥

(29)

पानाशनप्रसाधन-
सम्भुक्तसमस्तविश्वया शिवया ।
प्रलयोत्सवसरभसया
दृढमुपगूढं शिवं वन्दे ॥

(30)

परमेश्वरता जयत्यपूर्वा
तव विश्वेश यदीशितव्यशून्या ।
अपरापि तथैव ते ययेदं
जगदाभाति यथा तथा न भाति ॥

STOTRA NO. 17

(1)

अहो कोऽपि जयत्येष स्वादुः पूजामहोत्सवः ।
यतोऽमृतरसास्वादमस्त्रूण्यपि ददत्यलम् ॥

(2)

व्यापाराः सिद्धिदाः सर्वे ये त्वत्पूजापुरःसराः ।
भक्तानां त्वन्मयाः सर्वे स्वयं सिद्धय एव ते ॥

(3)

सर्वदा सर्वभावेषु युगपत्सर्वरूपिणम् ।
त्वामर्चयन्त्यविश्रान्तं ये ममैतेऽधिदेवताः ॥

(4)

ध्यानायासतिरस्कारसिद्धस्त्वत्स्पर्शनोत्सवः ।
पूजाविधिरिति ख्यातो भक्तानां स सदास्तु मे ॥

(5)

भक्तानां समतासारविषुवत्समयः सदा ।
त्वद्भावरसपीयूषरसेनैषां सदार्चनम् ॥

(6)

यस्यानारम्भपर्यन्तौ न च कालक्रमः प्रभो ।
पूजात्मासौ क्रिया तस्याः कर्तारस्त्वज्जुषः परम् ॥

(7)

ब्रह्मादीनामपीशास्ते ते च सौभाग्यभागिनः ।
येषां स्वप्नेऽपि मोहेऽपि स्थितस्त्वत्पूजनोत्सवः ॥

(8)

जपतां जुह्वतां स्नातां ध्यायतां न च केवलम् ।
भक्तानां भवदभ्यर्चामहो यावद्यदा तदा ॥

(9)

भवत्पूजासुधास्वादसम्भोगसुखिनः सदा ।
ब्रह्मादीनामथ ब्रह्ममुख्यानामस्ति कः समः ॥

(10)

जगत्क्षोभैकजनके भवत्पूजामहोत्सवे ।
यत्प्राप्यं प्राप्यते किंचिद्भुक्ता एव विदन्ति तत् ॥

(11)

त्वद्धाम्नि चिन्मये स्थित्वा षट्त्रिंशत्तत्त्वकर्मभिः ।
कायवाक्चित्तचेष्टाद्यैरर्चये त्वां सदा विभो ॥

(12)

भवत्पूजामयासङ्गसम्भोगसुखिनो मम ।
प्रयातु कालः सकलोऽप्यनन्तोऽपीयदर्थये ॥

(13)

भवत्पूजामृतरसाभोगलम्पटता विभो ।
विवर्धतामनुदिनं सदा च फलतां मम ॥

(14)

जगद्विलयसञ्जातसुधैकरसनिर्भरे ।
त्वदब्धौ त्वां महात्मानमर्चन्नासीय सर्वदा ॥

(15)

अशेषवासनाग्रन्थिविच्छेदसरलं सदा ।
मनो निवेद्यते भक्तैः स्वादु पूजाविधौ तव ॥

(16)

अधिष्ठायैव विषयानिमाः करणवृत्तयः ।
भक्तानां प्रेषयन्ति त्वत्पूजार्थममृतासवम् ॥

(17)

भक्तानां भक्तिसंवेगमहोष्मविवशात्मनाम् ।
कोऽन्यो निर्वाणहेतुः स्यात्त्वत्पूजामृतमज्जनात् ॥

(18)

सततं त्वत्पदाभ्यर्चासुधापानमहोत्सवः ।
त्वत्प्रसादैकसम्प्राप्तिहेतुर्मे नाथ कल्पताम् ॥

(19)

अनुभूयासमीशान प्रतिकर्म क्षणात्क्षणम् ।
भवत्पूजामृतापानमदास्वादमहामुदम् ॥

(20)

दृष्टार्थ एव भक्तानां भवत्पूजामहोद्यमः ।
तदैव यदसम्भाव्यं सुखमास्वादयन्ति ते ॥

(21)

यावन्न लब्धस्त्वत्पूजासुधास्वादमहोत्सवः ।
तावन्नास्वादितो मन्ये लवोऽपि सुखसम्पदः ॥

(22)

भक्तानां विषयान्वेषाभासायासाद्विनैव सा ।
अयत्नसिद्धं त्वद्धामस्थितिः पूजासु जायते ॥

(23)

न प्राप्यमस्ति भक्तानां नाप्येषामस्ति दुर्लभम् ।
केवलं विचरन्त्येते भवत्पूजामदोन्मदाः ॥

(24)

अहो भक्तिभरोदारचेतसां वरद त्वयि ।
श्लाघ्यः पूजाविधिः कोऽपि यो न यांञ्चाकलङ्कितः ॥

(25)

का न शोभा न को ह्लादः का समृद्धिर्न वापरा ।
को वा न मोक्षः कोऽप्येष महादेवो यदर्च्यते ॥

(26)

अन्तरुल्लसदच्छाच्छभक्तिपीयूषपोषितम् ।
भवत्पूजोपयोगाय शरीरमिदमस्तु मे ॥

(27)

त्वत्पादपूजासम्भोगपरतन्त्रः सदा विभो ।
भूयासं जगतामीश एकः स्वच्छन्दचेष्टितः ॥

(28)

त्वद्ध्यानदर्शनस्पर्शतृषि केषामपि प्रभो ।
जायते शीतलस्वादु भवत्पूजामहासरः ॥

(29)

यथा त्वमेव जगतः पूजासम्भोगभाजनम् ।
तथैव भक्तिमानेव पूजासम्भोगभाजनम् ॥

(30)

कोप्यसौ जयति स्वामिन्भवत्पूजामहोत्सवः ।
षट्त्रिंशतोऽपि तत्त्वानां क्षोभो यत्रोल्लसत्यलम् ॥

(31)

नमस्तेभ्यो विभो येषां भक्तिपीयूषवारिणा ।
पूज्यान्येव भवन्ति त्वत्पूजोपकरणान्यपि ॥

(32)

पूजारम्भे विभो ध्यात्वा मन्त्राधेयां त्वदात्मताम् ।
स्वात्मन्येव परे भवता मान्ति हर्षेण न क्वचित् ॥

(33)

राजलाभादिदोत्फुल्लैः कैश्चित्पूजामहोत्सवे ।
सुधासवेन सकला जगती संविभज्यते ॥

(34)

पूजामृतापानमयो येषां भोगः प्रतिक्षणम् ।
किं देवा उत मुक्तास्ते किं वा केऽप्येव ते जनाः ॥

(35)

पूजोपकरणीभूतविश्वावेशेन गौरवम् ।
अहो किमपि भक्तानां किमप्येव च लाघवम् ॥

(36)

पूजामयाक्षविक्षेपक्षोभादेवामृतोद्‌गमः ।
भक्तानां क्षीरजलधिक्षोभादिव दिवौकसाम् ॥

(37)

पूजां केचन मन्यन्ते धेनुं कामदुधामिव ।
सुधाधाराधिकरसां धयन्त्यन्तर्मुखाः परे ॥

(38)

भक्तानामक्षविक्षेपोऽप्येष संसारसम्मतः ।
उपनीय किमप्यन्तः पुष्णात्यर्चामहोत्सवम् ॥

(39)

भक्तिक्षोभवशादीश स्वात्मभूतेऽर्चनं त्वयि ।
चित्रं दैन्याय नो यावद्दीनतायाः परं फलम् ॥

(40)

उपचारपदं पूजा केषाञ्चित्त्वत्पदाप्तये ।
भक्तानां भवदैकात्म्यनिर्वृत्तिप्रसरस्तु सः ॥

(41)

अप्यसम्बद्धरूपार्चा भक्त्युन्मादनिरर्गलैः ।
वितन्यमाना लभते प्रतिष्ठां त्वयि कामपि ॥

(42)

स्वादुभक्तिरसास्वादस्तब्धीभूतमनश्च्युताम् ।
शम्भो त्वमेव ललितः पूजानां किल भाजनम् ॥

(43)

परिपूर्णानि शुद्धानि भक्तिमन्ति स्थिराणि च ।
भवत्पूजाविधौ नाथ साधनानि भवन्तु मे ॥

(44)

अशेषपूजासत्कोशे त्वत्पूजाकर्मणि प्रभो ।
अहो करणवृन्दस्य कापि लक्ष्मीर्विजृम्भते ॥

(45)

एषा पेशलिमा नाथ तवैव किल दृश्यते ।
विश्वेश्वरोऽपि भृत्यैर्यवर्च्यंसे यश्च लभ्यसे ॥

(46)

सदा मूर्त्तादमूर्त्ताद्वा भावाद्यद्वाप्यभावतः ।
उत्थेयान्मे प्रशस्तस्य भवत्पूजामहोत्सवः ॥

(47)

कामक्रोधाभिमानैस्त्वामुपहारीकृतैः सदा ।
येऽर्चयन्ति नमस्तेभ्यस्तेषां तुष्टोऽसि तत्त्वतः ॥

(48)

जयत्येष भवद्भक्तिभाजां पूजाविधिः परः ।
यस्तृणैः क्रियमाणोऽपि रत्नैरेवोपकल्पते ॥

STOTRA NO. 18

(1)

जगतोऽन्तरतो भवन्तमाप्त्वा
पुनरेतद्भवतोऽन्तराल्लभन्ते ।
जगदीश तवैव भक्तिभाजो
न हि तेषामिह दूरतोऽस्ति किञ्चित् ॥

(2)

क्वचिदेव भवान् क्वचिद्भवानी
सकलार्थक्रमगर्भिणी प्रधाना ।

परमार्थपदे तु नैव देव्या
भवतो नापि जगत्त्रयस्य भेदः ॥

(3)

नो जानते सुभगमप्यवलेपवन्तो
लोकाः प्रयत्नसुभगा निखिला हि भावाः।
चेतः पुनर्यदिदमुद्यतमप्यवैति
नैवात्मरूपमिह हा तदहो हतोऽस्मि ॥

(4)

भवन्मयस्वात्मनिवासलब्ध-
सम्पद्गुराभ्यर्चितयुष्मदङ्घ्रिः।
न भोजनाच्छादनमप्यजस्र-
मपेक्षते यस्तमहं नतोऽस्मि ॥

(5)

सदा भवद्देहनिवासस्वस्थो-
ऽप्यन्तः परं दह्यत एष लोकः।
तवेच्छया तत्कुरु मे यथात्र
त्वदर्चनानन्दमयो भवेयम् ॥

(6)

स्वरसोदितयुष्मदङ्घ्रिपद्म-
द्वयपूजामृतपानसक्तचित्तः।
सकलार्थचयेष्वहं भवेयं
सुखसंस्पर्शनमात्रलोकयात्रः ॥

(7)

सकलव्यवहारगोचरे
स्फुटमन्तः स्फुरति त्वयि प्रभो।
उपयान्त्यपयान्ति चानिशम्
मम वस्तूनि विभान्तु सर्वदा ॥

(8)

सततमेव तवैव पुरेऽथवा-
प्यरहितो विचरेयमहं त्वया।

क्षणलवोऽप्यथ मा स्म भवेत् स मे
न विजये ननु यत्र भवन्मयः ॥

(9)

भवदङ्घ्रिपरिस्रवत्सुशीता-
मृतपूरैर्भरिते समन्ततोऽपि ।
भवदर्चनसम्पदेह भक्ता-
स्तव संसारसरोऽन्तरे चरन्ति ॥

(10)

महामन्त्रतरुच्छायाशीतले त्वन्महावने ।
निजात्मनि सदा नाथ वसेयं तव पूजकः ॥

(11)

प्रतिवस्तु समस्तजीवतः
प्रतिभासि प्रतिभामयो यथा ।
मम नाथ तथा पुरः प्रथां
व्रज नेत्रत्रयशूलशोभितः ॥

(12)

अभिमानचरूपहारतो
ममताभक्तिभरेण कल्पितात् ।
परितोषगतः कदा भवान्
मम सर्वत्र भवेद् दृशः पदम् ॥

(13)

निवसन्परमामृताब्धिमध्ये
भवदर्चाविधिमात्रमग्नचित्तः ।
सकलं जनवृत्तमाचरेयं
रसयन्सर्वत एव किञ्चनापि ॥

(14)

भवदीयमिहास्तु वस्तु तत्त्वं
विवरीतुं क इवात्र पात्रमर्थे ।
इदमेव हि नामरूपचेष्टा-
द्यसमं ते हरते हरोऽसि यस्मात् ॥

(15)

शान्तये न सुखलिप्सुता मना-
ग्भक्तिसम्भृतमदेषु तैः प्रभोः ।
मोक्षमार्गणफलापि नार्थना
स्मर्यते हृदयहारिणः पुरः ॥

(16)

जागरेतरदशाथवा परा
यापि काचन मनागवस्थितेः ।
भक्तिभाजनजनस्य साखिला
त्वत्सनाथमनसो महोत्सवः ॥

(17)

भामनोऽक्षवलयस्य वृत्तयः
सर्वतः शिथिल वृत्तयोऽपि ताः ।
त्वामवाप्य दृढदीर्घसंविदो
नाथ भक्तिधनसोष्मणां कथम् ॥

(18)

न च विभिन्नमसृज्यत किञ्चिद-
स्यथ सुखेतरदत्र न निर्मितम् ।
अथ च दुःखि च भेदि च सर्वथा-
प्यसमविस्मयधाम नमोऽस्तु ते ॥

(19)

खरनिषेधखदामृतपूरणो-
च्छलितधौतविकल्पमलस्य मे ।
दलितदुर्जयसंशयवैरिण-
स्त्वदवलोकनमस्तु निरन्तरम् ॥

(20)

स्फुटमाविश मामथाविशेयं
सततं नाथ भवन्तमस्मि यस्मात् ।
रभसेन वपुस्तवैव साक्षा-
त्परमासत्तिगतः समर्चयेयम् ॥

(21)

त्वयि न स्तुतिशक्तिरस्ति कस्या-
प्यथवास्त्येव यतोऽतिसुन्दरोऽसि ।
सततं पुनरर्थितं ममैत-
द्यदविश्रान्ति विलोकयेयमीशम् ॥

STOTRA NO. 19

(1)

प्रार्थनाभूमिकातीतविचित्रफलदायकः ।
जयत्यपूर्ववृत्तान्तः शिवः सत्कल्पपादपः ॥

(2)

सर्ववस्तुनिचयैकनिधाना-
त्स्वात्मनस्त्वदखिलं किल लभ्यम् ।
अस्य मे पुनरसौ निज आत्मा
न त्वमेव घटसे परमास्ताम् ॥

(3)

ज्ञानकर्ममयचिद्वपुरात्मा
सर्वथैष परमेश्वर एव ।
स्याद्वपुस्तु निखिलेषु पदार्थे-
ष्वेषु नाम न भवेत्किमुतान्यत् ॥

(4)

विषमार्तिमुषानेन फलेन त्वद्दृगात्मना ।
अभिलीय यथा नाथ ममास्तु त्वन्मयी गतिः ॥

(5)

भवदमलचरणचिन्तारत्नलता-
लङ्कृता कदा सिद्धिः ।
सिद्धजनमानसानां विस्मयजननी
घटेत मम भवतः ॥

(6)

कर्हि नाथ विमलं मुखबिम्बं
तावकं समवलोकयितास्मि ।
यत्स्रवत्यमृतपूरमपूर्वं
यो निमज्जयति विश्वमशेषम् ॥

(7)

ध्यातमात्रमुदितं तव रूपं
कर्हि नाथ परमामृतपूरैः ।
पूरयेत्त्वदविभेदविमोक्षा-
ख्यातिदूरविवराणि सदा मे ॥

(8)

त्वदीयानुत्तररसासङ्गसन्त्यक्तचापलम् ।
नाद्यापि मे मनो नाथ कर्हि स्यावस्तु शीघ्रतः ॥

(9)

मा शुष्ककटुकान्येव परं सर्वाणि सर्वदा ।
तवोपहृत्य लब्धानि द्वन्द्वान्यप्यापतन्तु मे ॥

(10)

नाथ साम्मुख्यमायान्तु विशुद्धास्तव रश्मयः ।
यावत्कायमनस्तापतमोभिः परिलुप्यताम् ॥

(11)

देव प्रसीद यावन्मे त्वन्मार्गपरिपन्थिकाः ।
परमार्थमुषो वश्या भूयासुर्गुणतस्कराः ॥

(12)

त्वद्भक्तिसुधासारै-
र्मानसमापूर्यतां ममाशु विभो ।
यावदिमा उह्यन्तां
निःशेषासारवासनाः प्लुत्वा ॥

(13)

मोक्षदशायां भक्ति-
स्त्वयि कुत इव मर्त्यधर्मिणोऽपि न सा ।
राजति ततोऽनुरूपा
मारोपय सिद्धिभूमिकामज माम् ॥

(14)

सिद्धिलवलाभलुब्धं
मामवलेपेन मा विभो मंस्थाः ।
क्षामस्त्वद्भक्तिमुखे
प्रोल्लसदणिमादिपक्षतो मोक्षः ॥

(15)

दासस्य मे प्रसीदतु
भगवानेतावदेव ननु याचे ।
दाता त्रिभुवननाथो
यस्य न तन्मादृशां दृशो विषयः ॥

(16)

त्वद्वपुः स्मृतिसुधारसपूर्णे
मानसे तव पदाम्बुजयुग्मम् ।
मामके विकसदस्तु सदैव
प्रस्रवन्मधु किमप्यतिलोकम् ॥

(17)

अस्ति मे प्रभुरसौ जनकोऽथ
त्र्यम्बकोऽथ जननी च भवानी ।
न द्वितीय इह कोऽपि ममास्ती-
त्येव निर्वृततमो विचरेयम् ॥

STOTRA NO. 20

(1)

नाथं त्रिभुवननाथं भूतिसितं त्रिनयनं त्रिशूलधरम् ।
उपवीतीकृतभोगिनमिन्दुकलाशेखरं वन्दे ॥

(2)

नौमि निजतनुविनिस्सरदंशुकपरिवेषधवलपरिधानम् ।
विलसत्कपालमालाकल्पितनृत्तोत्सवाकल्पम् ॥

(3)

वन्दे तान् दैवतं येषां हरश्चेष्टा हरोचिताः ।
हरैकप्रवणाः प्राणाः सदा सौभाग्यसद्मनाम् ॥

(4)

क्रीडितं तव महेश्वरतायाः पृष्ठतोऽन्यदिदमेव यथैतत् ।
इष्टमात्रघटितेष्ववदानेष्वात्मना परमुपायमुपैमि ॥

(5)

त्वद्धाम्नि विश्ववन्द्येऽस्मिन्नियति क्रीडने सति ।
तव नाथ कियान् भूयान्नानन्दरससम्भवः ॥

(6)

कथं स सुभगो मा भूद्यो गौर्या वल्लभो हरः ।
हरोऽपि मा भूदथ किं गौर्याः परमवल्लभः ॥

(7)

ध्यानामृतमयं यस्य स्वात्ममूलमनश्वरम् ।
संविल्लतास्तथारूपास्तस्य कस्यापि सत्तरोः ॥

(8)

भक्तिकण्डूसमुल्लासावसरे परमेश्वर ।
महानिकषपाषाणस्थूणा पूजैव जायते ॥

(9)

सदा सृष्टिविनोदाय सदा स्थितिसुखासिने ।
सदा त्रिभुवनाहारतृप्ताय स्वामिने नमः ॥

(10)

न क्वापि गत्वा हित्वापि न किञ्चिदिदमेव ये ।
भव्यं त्वद्धाम पश्यन्ति भव्यास्तेभ्यो नमो नमः ॥

(11)

भक्तिलक्ष्मीसमृद्धानां किमन्यदुपयाचितम् ।
एतया वा दरिद्राणां किमन्यदुपयाचितम् ॥

(12)

दुःखान्यपि सुखायन्ते विषमप्यमृतायते ।
मोक्षायते च संसारो यत्र मार्गः स शाङ्करः ॥

(13)

मूले मध्येऽवसाने च नास्ति दुःखं भवज्जुषाम् ।
तथापि वयमीशान सीदामः कथमुच्यताम् ॥

(14)

ज्ञानयोगादिनान्येषामप्यपेक्षितुमर्हति ।
प्रकाशः स्वैरिणामेव भवान् भक्तिमतां प्रभो ॥

(15)

भक्तानां नार्तयो नास्त्यप्याध्यानं स्वात्मनस्तव ।
तथाप्यस्ति शिवेत्येतत्किमप्येषां बहिर्मुखे ॥

(16)

सर्वाभासावभासो यो विमर्शवलितोऽखिलम् ।
अहमेतदिति स्तौमि तां क्रियाशक्तिमीश ते ॥

(17)

वर्तन्ते जन्तवोऽशेषा अपि ब्रह्मेन्द्रविष्णवः ।
ग्रसमानास्ततो वन्दे देव विश्वं भवन्मयम् ॥

(18)

सतो विनाशसम्बन्धान्मत्परं निखिलं मृषा ।
एवमेवोद्यते नाथ त्वया संहारलीलया ॥

(19)

ध्यातमात्रमुपतिष्ठत एव
त्वद्वपुर्वरद भक्तिधनानाम् ।
अप्यचिन्त्यमखिलाद्भुतचिन्ता-
कर्तृतां प्रति च ते विजयन्ते ॥

(20)

तावकभक्तिरसासव-
सेकाविव सुखितमर्ममण्डलस्फुरितैः ।
नृत्यति वीरजनो निशि
वेतालकुलैः कृतोत्साहः ॥

(21)

आरब्धा भवबभिनुति-
रमुना येनाङ्कुकेन मम शम्भो ।
तेनापर्यन्तमिमं कालं
वृढमखिलमेव भविषीष्ट ॥

GLOSSARY

Advaita : non-dualism.

Adhvā : path, course.

Aṇimā : One of the eight *siddhis* which enables a *yogī* to become infinitesimally small.

Anugraha : divine grace.

Āgamas : Revealed texts handed over for ages from teacher to pupil. They are known as tantras, and are held in great esteem as authorities on spiritual subjects.

Ātman : self.

Ānanda : bliss.

Āṇava Mala : limitation of the power of will. Impuriy in the form of innate ignorance which makes an individual imagine himself to be imperfect.

Āṇavopāya : Spiritual discipline in which a seeker uses his own senses and *prāṇas* for self-realization. It includes rituals, worship of images and *japa* etc.

Ābhāsa : reflection, idea.

Icchā : will, desire, power of will.

Īśvara : The term means Lord. It is a state of universal Consciousness below that of *Sadāśiva* in which the idea of thisness is clear.

Unmanā : State of super-consciousness in which the mind is dissolved.

Unmeṣa : unfoldment; *dhāraṇā* in which a *yogī* concentrates on the junction point between two thoughts in an effort to attain unqualified *samādhi.*

Unmīlana samādhi : That form of *samādhi* in which the whole world appears to the *yogī* as *Śiva* himself without closing his eyes.

Kaivalyam : *Puruṣa* remaining aloof from *prakṛti.* This is the Sāṅkhya conception of liberation.

Kañcuka : covering.

Kāla : temporal order, sense of succession.

Kalā : limitation of the power of action.

Kālakūṭa : Deadly poison obtained from the ocean of milk and swallowed by Lord *Śiva* in order to avoid universal holocaust.

Kārma mala : limitation of the power of action.

Kuṇḍalinī : literally the coiled one. Cosmic energy lying dormant in the *mūlādhāra cakra* at the base of the spinal column. When awakened by *yogic* practices it moves upwards through the central channel of *suṣumṇā* till it reaches the crown of the head becoming one with *Śiva* in the *sahasrāra cakra*. The *yogī* then attains his goal of self-realization.

Kriyā : The power of action.

Kriyā Śakti : One of the powers of the Lord. The power of the Lord to assume any form. Power of activity.

Gaurī : The consort of the Lord in His personal form. Divine Mother.

Guṇas : attributes. Constituents of *prakṛti*, that is, *Sattva*, *rajas* and *tamas* which are derivatives respectively of *jñāna*, *icchā* and *kriyā Śaktis*.

Cakra : Centre of *prāṇic* activities.

cit : Absolute consciousness.

Japa : Constant repetition of a *mantra*.

Jāgrata : waking state.

Jaḍa samādhi : This is a state of negative experience from which it is not possible to return into normal consciousness till the end of the cosmic cycle. Individuals in this state have no physical body and are almost insentient.

Jñāna : knowledge, realization.

Jīvanmukta : One liberated in one's life time.

Tantras : revealed texts of divine origin.

Tanmātras : Rudimentary elements as distinguished from the gross forms of sound, touch, colour, taste and odour.

Tattva : literally 'thatness'. The basic categories of universal manifestation. These are thirty six in number.

Tāmasa : Obscuring force of *prakṛti*.

Turīyā : the fourth state of consciousness beyond those of waking, dream and deep sleep.

Turīyātītā : A state of consciousness beyond the fourth. It is the state of *Parama-Śiva* in which nothing is experienced apart from the self. The mind gets dissolved in the process.

Dāsyam : The state of a servant. In the cult of *bhakti* a devotee invokes *Śiva* as the master and considers himself as his humble servant. This is indicative of humility on the part of a devotee.

Devarṣis : A class of divine sages of whom Nārada is one.

Duḥkhānta : cessation of pain.

Dhyāna : meditation.

Dhṛti : perseverence, firmness of mind, fortitude.

Nāḍīs : Subtle channels for the flow of *prāṇas*.

Nityodita samādhi : Highest form of *samādhi* that remains unbroken in all conditions of life. It is also known as *sahaja* samādhi.

Nirvikalpa samādhi : Super-conscious thought-free state in which the *yogī* is not aware of anything other than the self.

Nirvikalpa jñāna : indeterminate cognition.

Nimīlana samādhi : Meditative state in which the *yogi* is not aware of the outside world. This is an introvert form of *samādhi* in which the senses remain closed to the world outside.

Niyati : One of the five *kañcukas* of *Māyā* responsible for fixed results from fixed causes.

Pati : Śiva

Pañca kṛtyas : Five acts of the Lord, that is creation, preservation, dissolution, grace and obscuration.

Parama Śiva : the ultimate Reality.

Parā Vāk : Cosmic ideation holding within it all forms of knowledge, spiritual as well as mundane.

Paśu : An embodied soul bound by *Māyā*.

Paśyantī : This is a materialization of *parā vāk* in which the words are not different from their meaning, and corresponds to the state of *Sadāśiva* in which the idea of this-ness is present in a vague form.

Puruṣa : the self.

Pratyabhijñā : recognition.

Prakṛti : The primordial source of objectivity in relation to puruṣa, the experient. It is the state of identity of the three *guṇas*.

Prakāśa : light.

Pramāṇas : means of knowledge.

Pramātā : literally experient. These are seven in number, viz, *Śiva, mantra maheśvaras, mantreśvaras, vidyeśvaras, vijñānākalās, pralayākalās* and *sakalās* corresponding to various levels of consciousness.

Pratyāhāra : The practice of withdrawing all senses from their respective objects. This is the fifth step in the eight-limbed *yoga* of Patañjali.

Prāṇa : vital energy.

Prārabdha : The accumulated *karma* that has already started bearing fruit.

Pralayākalās : Limited subjects, whose consciousness shines in relation to *Śūnya*. They remain in a state of unconsciousness till the end of the universe. They have got two impurities of *āṇava* and *māyīya*. They are without physical bodies. Also called *pralayakevalins.*

Bhakti : devotion.

Buddhi : intellect.

Bhavānī : One of the names of the Divine Mother, *Parā Śakti*, Consort of *Bhava*.

Bhava : another name of *Śiva*.

Brahmā : the Lord of creation.

Brahmarṣis : Sages of Brāhmaṇic origin.

Māyā : The power of obscuration of the Lord responsible for appearance of unreal things as real and *vice versa*.

Māyīya mala : Limitation of the power of knowledge which brings about the sense of differentiation.

Mala : impurity.

Mantra : A mystic formula for repetition during *japa*.

Mantra Maheśvaras : Experients of the state of *Sadāśiva*, having supreme I-consciousness with a hazy notion of this-ness.

Mantreśvaras : Experients of the stage of *Iśvara* in which the notion of this-ness becomes clear.

Maheśvara : another name of Śiva, omnipotent.

Mahātmā : a great soul.

Madhyamā : Sound in its subtle form as existing in the mind

in which words and their meaning are differentiated before being uttered through various points in the vocal organ.

Mokṣa
Mukti : } liberation

Munis : Sages intent on exploring the ultimate Truth.

Yoga : Spiritual endeavour to become united with the higher self.

Yogī : One who is seeking to attain union with the Supreme.

Rudra : another name of *Śiva.*

Rāga : Attachment for one thing to the exclusion of another. One of the five *kañcuka*s of *Māyā*..

Rajas: Principle of motion. One of the three constituents of *prakṛti.* Its predominance causes avarice and attachment in man.

Līlā : sport.

Vaikharī : articulate speech.

Vāsanās : tendencies of the mind existing in latent form.

Vāsudeva : Lord Kṛṣṇa, the son of Vasudeva. All-pervading Lord of the universe.

Vikalpa : idea, thought.

Vidyā : limited knowledge. One of the five *kañcukas* of *Māyā.*

Vidyeśvaras : Experients of the stage of *Śuddha Vidyā.* Also called *mantras.*

Vijñānākalās: Experients of the stage between *Māyā* and *Śuddha Vidyā.* They retain a single impurity of *āṇava.* They have full awareness but lack the power of activity.

Vibhūti : super-normal power, splendour.

Vimarśa : power of deliberation and freedom of the Lord, *Svātantrya Śakti.*

Viṣṇu : Lord of preservation in Hindu pantheon.

Vyutthāna : normal consciousness as against *samādhi.*

Vṛttis : modifications of the mind.

Vismaya Mudrā : Final leap in spiritual development. A state of supreme bewilderment in which a *yogī* is struck by new experiences flowing into his consciousness, and is stunned to discover the whole universe as nothing but Śiva, his own self.

Śakti : dynamic aspect of Śiva. Power of freedom of the Lord.

Śaktipāta : descent of Śakti; divine grace.

Śāktopāya : One of the means to self-realization through knowledge and meditation on the self as '*Śivo'ham*' (I am Śiva). It is also called Jñānopāya because mental activity plays an important role in it.

Śāmbhavopāya : Sudden emergence of Śiva consciousness as a result of intense meditation and divine grace.

Śivadāsa : Śiva's servant. Devotees consider God as the Master and prefer to call themselves as His humble servants.

Śivo'ham: lit. 'I am Śiva'. This is a *mantra* repeated by aspirants in order to cultivate awareness of the self as distinct from the body and other coverings.

Śuddha adhvā : The pure path comprising first five *tattvas* of universal consciousness.

Śuddha vidyā : Fifth *tattva* in universal consciousness. At this stage I-ness and this-ness are equally prominent.

Śūnya bhūmi : A state of negative experience generally faced by *yogīs* when the mind becomes totally quiescent as a result of yogic practices. It is a sort of wilderness standing between the two worlds of consciousness and that of senses. The mind becomes blank without any tangible gain. One must go beyond this in order to have positive experience of the ultimate Reality.

Satsaṅga : Association of good and godly persons.

Sādhanā : spiritual effort.

Sādhaka : one given to spiritual practice.

Sannyāsa : renunciation, the institution of monks.

Sattva : one of the constituents of *prakṛti*. Its predominance is productive of knowledge and tranquility.

Sakalās : Limited subjects affected by all the three *malas*; they identify themselves with physical bodies and lack knowledge of the self.

Samāveśa
Samādhi :
Samāpatti } Superconscious experience of the ultimate Reality.

Saṃskāras : Residual traces of past actions in the mind.

Savikalpa samādhi : State of *samādhi* in which the strain of mind is still felt in a subtle form.

Savikalpa jñāna : determinate cognition.

Sadāśiva : The third *tattva* in universal Consciousness. At this stage the idea of this-ness rises for the first time in a hazy form while I-consciousness predominates.

Sambodhi : Enlightenment that came to Buddha after heroic struggle.

Samanā : The state of *jñānīs* who have still some *vāsanās* left in them.

Samanaskas : *jñānīs* of the above description.

Siddhi : perfection; attainment of oneness with the Lord.

Siddhis : Super-natural powers attained through the practice of *yoga*.

Siddha : a spiritually perfect person.

Suṣupti : state of dreamless sleep.

Suṣumṇā : Central channel in the spinal column extending from the base of the spine to the crown of the head. It is through this *nāḍī* that *Kuṇḍalinī* rises upwards towards the crown of the head.

Stotras : hymns.

Svātantrya Śakti : power of freedom of the Lord.

Svapna svātantryam : The capability of maintaining self-awareness even in the state of dreams.

Hara : another name of *Śiva*. Other names are Śaṅkara, Śarva, Śambhu etc.

INDEX OF SANSKRIT VERSES

ADDENDA & CORRIGENDA

Page	*Line*	*For*	*Read*
2	9	disarray.	disarray after he gave up his mortal coil.
5	34	eastern	western
8	1	moment	movement
—	12	conational	actional
14	11	fulfilment. At the	fulfilment the
18	24	but as a temple	but considers it as a temple
24	15	into	onto
28	14	first, of these	first of these
—	20	unless knots	unless these knots
30	39	her	her heart's
55	24	on whose, tongue	on whose tongue
65	28	O Lord.	O Lord,
80	17	coutenance	countenance
83	29	worhty	worthy
104	9	सुकदप्यसो	सकृदप्यसो
111	15/16	ववस्वां श्चन्द्रमः	विवस्वां श्चन्द्रमः
122	9	हासील्लासित	हासोल्लासित
136	15	सद्वितीयक	सद्द्वितीयक
142	10	लीक	लोक
153	15	त्वद्दगात्मना	त्वदृगात्मना
170	27A	भवङ्ग	भवदङ्ग